Thanks ~for
sors?
s to(

MW00800070

WILLOW BROOK SDA CHURCH
8916 MAPLEVILLE ROAD
BOONSBORO, MD 21713
301-797-8808
WWW.WILLOWBROOK.CHURCH

Radical Evidence

Also by Derek J. Morris:

The Radical Prayer

Radical Protection

The Radical Teachings of Jesus

To order, call 1-800-765-6955.

Visit us at

www.AutumnHousePublishing.com

for information on other Autumn House® products.

Radical Evidence

*Compelling Testimonies About Jesus
From Transformed Witnesses*

Derek J. Morris

Autumn
House® Publishing
www.autumnhousepublishing.com
A Division of REVIEW AND HERALD® PUBLISHING
Since 1861

Autumn House® titles may be purchased in bulk for educational, business, fund-raising, or sales promotional use. For information, please e-mail SpecialMarkets@reviewand herald.com.

Autumn House® Publishing publishes biblically based materials for spiritual, physical, and mental growth and Christian discipleship.

The author assumes full responsibility for the accuracy of all facts and quotations as cited in this book.

Unless otherwise indicated, Scripture references are from the *Holy Bible, New International Version*. Copyright © 1973, 1978, 1984, 2011 by Biblica, Inc. Used by permission. All rights reserved worldwide.

Texts credited to NKJV are from the New King James Version. Copyright © 1979, 1980, 1982 by Thomas Nelson, Inc. Used by permission. All rights reserved.

This book was
Edited by Gerald Wheeler
Copyedited by James Cavil
Designed by Emily Ford/Review & Herald® Design Center
Cover design by Et Design
Cover photos by ©Thinkstock.com
Typeset: Clearface 10/14.5

PRINTED IN U.S.A.

18 17 16 15 14 13   5 4 3 2 1

Library of Congress Cataloging-in-Publication Data

Morris, Derek John, 1954-
  Radical evidence : compelling testimony about Jesus from transformed witnesses / Derek J. Morris.
       pages cm.
  Includes bibliographical references and index.

1. Christian converts--Biography. 2. Jesus Christ--Biblical teaching. I. Title.
  BV4930.M67 2013
  248.2'460922--dc23

2012049346

ISBN 978-0-8127-0514-0 (alk. hardcover)
ISBN 978-0-8127-0515-7 (alk. paperback)

This book is

to those whose lives have been transformed through a life-

changing encounter with their Lord and Savior Jesus Christ.

The word of their testimony has overcome the evil one and shed

light in the midst of the darkness.

With them, and the saints of all ages, we declare the praises of

Him who called us "out of darkness into His marvelous light"

(1 Peter 2:9, NKJV).

The identity of Jesus is no secondary matter.
If Jesus is not the divine Son of God
and merely a wise religious teacher (or worse, a fake),
His offer of eternal life has no substance at all.
In Radical Evidence *you will discover who Jesus really is*
and find answers that will satisfy your intellect
and warm your heart.

—Mark Finley, Evangelist

Acknowledgments

I want to express my appreciation to the numerous individuals who have provided encouragement and assistance in completing this book:

To Nancy Costa, Kimberly Bobenhausen Harris, Monika Bliss Morris, Eve Parker, and Nancy Vasquez—who offered invaluable feedback in the shaping and editing of the manuscript.

To my beloved wife, Bodil—whose wholehearted devotion to Jesus as Savior and Lord has inspired me, and whose prayers in the name of Jesus have sustained me.

To those whose compelling testimonies are included in this book—who are "not ashamed of the gospel, because it is the power of God that brings salvation to everyone who believes" (Romans 1:16).

Each one of the individuals, along with others unnamed, encouraged me to follow the clear promptings of the Holy Spirit in the preparation of this book.

Most of all, I give thanks and honor to Jesus, who is so much more than just another great teacher or another holy prophet—He is the Christ, the Son of God, our Savior and Lord.

Contents

INTRODUCTION

CHAPTER 1 / THE TESTIMONY OF YASMIN SULTANA,
AN ORTHODOX MUSLIM FROM KOLKATA, INDIA

13

CHAPTER 2 / THE TESTIMONY OF PAUL RATSARA,
AN ANCESTOR WORSHIPPER FROM RURAL MADAGASCAR

31

CHAPTER 3 / THE TESTIMONY OF CLEOPAS,
A DISCIPLE OF JESUS

43

CHAPTER 4 / THE TESTIMONY OF MOSES

59

CHAPTER 5 / THE TESTIMONY OF THE PROPHETS

75

CHAPTER 6 / THE TESTIMONY OF THE PSALMISTS

87

CHAPTER 7 / THE TESTIMONY OF SHAHBAZ,
A SHIITE MUSLIM FROM TEHRAN, IRAN

97

CHAPTER 8 / THE TESTIMONY OF CLIFF GOLDSTEIN,
A SECULAR JEW FROM MIAMI BEACH, FLORIDA
111

EPILOGUE
121

DISCUSSION QUESTIONS FOR SMALL-GROUP STUDY

Introduction

Do you know the truth about Jesus of Nazareth? Was He just another great teacher? *Or* another self-proclaimed holy prophet, as some suggest? The apostle John concluded his inspired testimony of the life and teachings of Jesus by declaring, "Jesus performed many other signs in the presence of his disciples, which are not recorded in this book. But these are written that you may believe that Jesus is the Messiah, the Son of God, and that by believing you may have life in his name" (John 20:30, 31).

I have written *Radical Evidence* with the same purpose in mind. If Jesus is indeed the Messiah, the Son of God, that fact has eternal implications for your life and mine. Jesus boldly declared His desire for each one of us: "I have come that they may have life, and have it to the full" (John 10:10). If He is who He claimed to be, His promise has value both in this life and on into eternity.

Radical Evidence includes compelling testimonies from the twenty-first century as well as Scripture. You can read the chapters sequentially or start with any one that catches your attention.

I pray that you will be eternally blessed as you consider the radical evidence concerning Jesus of Nazareth. Then go with joy and share the life-changing truth you have embraced.

1

The Testimony of Yasmin Sultana

An Orthodox Muslim From Kolkata, India

Yasmin is completely convinced that Jesus is more than a great teacher, more than just another prophet. She has trusted her life into His care now and for eternity, and experienced His presence and power in her life. But there was a time she had not even heard the name of Jesus.

Growing Up in Kolkata

Yasmin grew up in an orthodox Muslim family. Ethnic Bengali, they lived in Kolkata, in the eastern part of India. Her parents had a humble beginning in their life together. After getting married and moving into the city, her father started a business and eventually became quite successful. Tragically, their first two sons died at birth, so when Yasmin was born, her parents welcomed her as a great treasure.

As part of an orthodox Muslim family, Yasmin received training in the traditions of Islam. Taught to pray five times a day, she read regularly from the Quran. The Sultana family spoke Bengali at home, but all prayers and Quran readings were in Arabic. Yasmin began her *namaz,* her daily prayers in Arabic, when she was 8 years old. She recited the prayers even if she didn't understand them. Also she began her directed reading through the Quran. All Muslim girls must complete the Quran by the age of 9, and once they finish it, they start through it again. Yasmin read through the Quran at least three times. She also began fasting during Ramadan.[1]

While it is not mandatory to memorize the Quran, a person who has committed it to memory (a Hafiz) has earned high respect in the Muslim community. Yasmin's parents paid for a Hafiz to come to their home and help her read through the Quran.

Today, as Yasmin looks back on her life, she can see God's leading even when she was a young girl. All her cousins went to Muslim schools, but Yasmin's mother wanted her to attend a Christian school in Kolkata so that she could learn to speak English. She enrolled at St. Augustine's Day School when she was 6 years old and attended nursery, lower kindergarten, upper kindergarten, class 1, and all the way through class 12. The students used to pray the Lord's Prayer every day at the school.[2] Yasmin was still praying her *namaz* and reading the Quran, but she was also learning more about Christianity.

Unanswered Questions

Her study of the Quran raised many questions in her mind: *Why this? What is the meaning of that?* Her parents got tired of hiring and rehiring a Hafiz to guide her through the Quran because it took such a long time—she would stop reading to ask questions. The typical answer she would get from the Hafiz was: "We don't have to know the meaning."

But Yasmin would insist, "No, I want to know the meaning. Tell me the meaning." Because she asked so many questions, her instructors regarded her as a bad student of the Quran.

When Yasmin was 16 years old, she decided to find answers to her questions and bought a translation of the Quran by Allama Yusuf Ali. When that did not help, she stopped reading the Quran and saying her *namaz*. While it angered her parents, they did not force her to continue. She had fulfilled the minimum requirement of reading through the Quran once. Although Yasmin was excelling academically, she still felt a hunger in her soul.

Free Food

Hearing about Jesus at school, especially at Christmas, Yasmin began to ask who He was. After completing class 10 and taking her government examinations, she had a three-month break from school. She decided to join with a group of six other classmates for some window-shopping and looking around the city of Kolkata. One of her friends noticed a sign for a seminar nearby that provided a free lunch. The seminar was in a building on one of the busy streets in Kolkata. A sign outside said "REVIVAL," but they had no idea what that meant. The girls went inside and ate the free food. After lunch the speaker started a presentation about ancient civilizations. Yasmin had no clue what he was talking about. The girls had missed the first part of the seminar and felt totally lost. Then the man started talking about the Bible and how its prophecies have been fulfilled. He showed evidence from ancient history. For example, he quoted the prophecy about the destruction of the city of Tyre: "They will destroy the walls of Tyre and pull down her towers; I will scrape away her rubble and make her a bare rock" (Ezekiel 26:4). Next he informed his audience about the prophecy regarding the great city of Babylon: "Thorns will overrun her citadels, nettles and brambles her strongholds. She will become a haunt for jackals, a home for owls" (Isaiah 34:13). Then he showed that both prophecies had come to pass. Yasmin became interested in what he was presenting.

Some of her friends wanted to leave after the free lunch, but she decided to stay, and remained until later that afternoon. When the seminar ended, there were people standing at the door. Yasmin had no idea that she was in a Christian church. The people shook her hand and said, "Please come tomorrow!"

"Oh, you have this meeting again tomorrow?"

"Yes, it's all week!" The Christian pastor was presenting a series on the book of Revelation.

Yasmin could not have attended during the school year, but it was summer break, so she said, "OK. Fine."

The next day her friends decided to go window-shopping again. "No, I don't want to go," Yasmin told them. "I want to attend that meeting."

"What's wrong with you?" they demanded. "Are you just going for the free food?"

"Uh, sort of," she replied. But she was searching for a different kind of food—spiritual food to satisfy the hunger of her soul.

She attended the seminar all week with about 100 other participants. The meetings began every day at 9:00 a.m. and continued until 4:30 or 5:00 p.m. The intensive study had at last begun to answer many of her questions. The presenter was teaching from the Bible. Yasmin took careful notes of every word the pastor said. At the end of the week they had a quiz, and she got the highest score! The prize was a small red Bible— her first one. She still has it today and treasures it. But she had to take it home secretly, because her parents had no idea what she was doing.

Yasmin discovered during that seminar that the Bible is

a reliable testimony, inspired by God. That was an important lesson for an orthodox Muslim. She also learned more about Jesus. It wasn't hard for her to accept Him as a prophet, because Muslims regard Jesus as one, but she considered Him as just one of many prophets, with Muhammad as the greatest of all. It was challenging to hear the teaching about Jesus as God. So when Yasmin received that small red Bible, she started reading it.

Putting the Words of Jesus to the Test

She read the promise of Jesus, "And I will do whatever you ask in my name, so that the Father may be glorified in the Son. You may ask me for anything in my name, and I will do it" (John 14:13, 14). So Yasmin decided to put the words of Jesus to the test. In India, women often wear open-toed sandals, and many times hers would break. She decided to pray a simple prayer: "Lord, let my sandal never be broken again." While it may have appeared to be an insignificant request, it was a prayer from her heart, and she presented it "in the name of Jesus." Her sandals have never broken again. God has been faithful to a humble prayer offered in the name of Jesus. It still brings tears to her eyes when she tells her story. Jesus met Yasmin right where she was. He revealed Himself to her as more than just a great teacher or prophet—as the true Messiah, the Son of God.

Yasmin prayed more prayers in the name of Jesus, and

God kept His promise to her. One time she had diligently prepared for a topic in biology and wanted the teacher to ask her a question in class. Timid, she didn't often speak up. So she prayed, "Lord, when the teacher comes to class today, I would like him to ask a question no one else can answer. Then, help him to notice me." During the biology class the teacher raised a difficult question on the topic under discussion to the class of 80 students. "Can anyone answer it?" Then he pointed to Yasmin. "OK, you. Do you know the answer?" Although it involved the difficult subject of mitosis and meiosis, she knew the correct answer. Her prayer was answered in exactly the way she had asked in the name of Jesus. While they might have been just small prayers, she saw their fulfillment as compelling evidence that God was leading her.

Public Confession of Faith in Jesus

After attending church for about a year, Yasmin decided it was time to make a personal commitment to Jesus Christ as her Messiah, her Savior, and her Lord. She asked an elder of the church if she could be baptized as a public confession of her newfound faith in Jesus, but she was met with resistance. People were afraid of the trouble that might occur if a young Muslim woman became a Christian. It might lead to a violent public reaction. The church members were happy for her to attend, but they did not encourage her when she asked to be baptized. Yasmin felt discouraged, but before giving up completely, she decided to speak to the pastor. He was the same person who had conducted the seminar a year earlier. "Pastor, I want to be baptized," she told him.

He looked into her eyes and said, "Are you sure?"

"Yes, sir. I'm very sure. No matter what happens, I am ready."

"Yasmin, for one week I want you to pray the way you have been praying, in your own words in the name of Jesus. I will pray too. After this one week, if God gives me the conviction that He has placed a call on you, and you still feel the conviction that you want to belong to Him, then no matter what happens, I will baptize you. I will take the consequences." It was also risky for him, but his willingness to pray about her situation in the name of Jesus gave her hope. After a week Yasmin went back to the pastor. "I will baptize you," he told her.

She was baptized January 6, 2001, after she completed high school. By this time her parents knew she was attending a Christian church but did not know she had made a public confession of her faith in Jesus as her Messiah. Yasmin wanted to tell her parents because the joy of the Lord was bubbling up inside of her, but she sensed God saying to her, "Not now." Although she never lied to her parents, she just didn't tell them everything that was happening in her heart. One time they asked her, "Why are you going to church?"

"They are a nice group of people," she replied. "I'm not doing drugs or partying." Even then she was aware of God working on her parents. What Muslim family would be silent if their daughter was attending a Christian church? But her parents never prevented her from going.

Disowned by Her Family

Everything turned upside down when it came time to continue her education. Her father made arrangements for her to attend a prestigious college. He wanted her to study science and ultimately go into medicine. "Everything is ready," he announced. "The fees are paid and the papers are prepared. Let's go."

That is when she told him, "No, I don't want to study science; I want to study religion."

He laughed. "What did you say?"

"I want to study religion," she replied calmly.

"What are you talking about?"

That's when Yasmin told him she had been baptized as a follower of Jesus and desired to study the Christian religion. Her father pushed himself away from the table and stood. Looking straight at her, he said, "You did what?" Then he silently walked away from the table.

"What did you do?" her mother questioned. Yasmin tried to explain, but her mother interrupted, "Have you gone mad?" That was the end of their family discussion.

After a week of silence, Yasmin's father said to her, "Were you joking? Has your madness gone now? Are you sane now?"

"Dad, I wasn't joking. I'm serious."

He went into her room, came out with a suitcase, and said, "OK, here are your things. But remember, once you leave this place, never in your life think that you can ever come back."

Yasmin didn't know what to do. She didn't have any money and had been sheltered and protected all her life. So she prayed in the name of Jesus: "Lord, what shall I do?" She felt God's presence. Her father told her, "Leave, and from today your parents are dead. Don't ever turn your face toward us again."

In that time of crisis God gave Yasmin strength. He was there. She thought, *I trust God. I'm not going to focus on how I'm going to get money, how I am going to go to school, or where I will stay.* The following promise became real in her life: "Trust in the Lord with all your heart and lean not on your own understanding; in all your ways submit to him, and he will make your paths straight" (Proverbs 3:5, 6).

As her father escorted Yasmin out the door, her mother tried to intervene: "Where are you taking her? She is just a young girl. Where will she go?" But her father said, "Don't interfere. She has made her decision. Tell her to get out of my house. There is no place for a *kafir* [an unbeliever] in my house."[3]

Trip to Spicer Memorial College

Yasmin took her suitcase and went to the church. When she told the pastor what had happened, he gave her a check for 25,000 rupees and a train ticket to Pune so that she could begin her studies in religion at Spicer Memorial College. She never learned where the money came from—only that God had provided. It is 2,280 miles (3,700 kilometers) from Kolkata to Spicer Memorial College, on the outskirts of Pune. The train was scheduled to arrive in Pune at 3:00 a.m. Traveling alone and being out late at night was not something a young woman in India should do. Someone could have abducted, killed, or sold her to a brothel. All kinds of harm could have come to her, but Yasmin took the ticket, boarded the train, and arrived 36 hours later at the Pune train station. She knew no one there.

As she waited at the train station, she prayed. Not only did she not know what to do—she didn't even know where Spicer Memorial College was. Then a tall slender man approached her and asked, "Where are you going, my child?"

"I want to go to Spicer Memorial College."

Smiling, he reached for her suitcase. "OK, I will take you." Yasmin followed, even though she had never met him before. It was her first time outside of the city of Kolkata, but she had peace in her heart. She knew God was there.

The driver took her in his auto rickshaw about 12.5 miles (20 kilometers) from the train station right to the front door of the girls' dormitory on the campus of Spicer Memorial College. If he had dropped her anywhere else on the campus, she would have been lost. "Here you are," he said with a smile. As Yasmin recounted her story to me, tears filled her eyes: "My God is good! My God is very, very good."

Yasmin studied and worked at Spicer Memorial College for the next seven years, and several times she tried to reconnect with that kind driver. Although she will always remember his face, she was never able to find him. Yasmin is convinced God sent him there in answer to her prayer in the name of Jesus.

Times of Discouragement

During her first semester at Spicer Yasmin faced a major challenge. Someone made a false accusation against her, and she became very discouraged. Back in her room, she started crying. "Lord, is this what You brought me here for?" Thinking that she had made a mistake coming all the way from Kolkata, she now wanted to go home. She even contacted some of her friends in Kolkata to obtain some money for her train ticket.

In the midst of her struggle with discouragement, Yasmin received a message from the vice president for student affairs. He asked her to his office. "You are Yasmin? You have come all the way from Kolkata? I hear that you want to go home."

"Yes, sir," she replied. Starting to cry, she shared with him the whole story of the false accusation. Then she said, "Sir, this is not what I left my parents for. I think I made a mistake. I don't belong here."

After listening attentively, he then said to her, "Yasmin, God knows what He has in store for you. Don't let His plans fail." Those words touched her heart. *It's true,* she thought to herself. *God has led me this far. Why am I doubting Him now?*

New strength and courage filled her. "You know, sir," she told the administrator, "you will see me finish my studies in religion and go out from here." Then they prayed together in the name of Jesus.

As Yasmin was about to leave the administrator's office, he said, "Yasmin, it is very easy to flow with the current, but it takes courage and God's strength to swim against the current. Don't forget that."

Blessings at Spicer

Yasmin became one of the most distinguished students at Spicer Memorial College. Before every examination she would pray, "Not in my strength, Lord, but in Your strength I go to write this exam. In the name of Jesus, amen." Yasmin was blessed. She received five academic awards and finished her undergraduate studies in religion and psychology with a grade point average (GPA) of 3.93. Then she completed her graduate studies in education with a perfect 4.0 GPA. "I didn't accomplish that in my own strength," she testified. "It was a miracle."

After two years away from home, she got a phone call from her father. The administration building had a general phone, and if students received phone calls someone would summon them on the loudspeaker system. When Yasmin heard her name announced, she thought, *Who is calling me? No one ever calls me.* She made her way to the administration building and picked up the phone. "*Assalamu alaikum* [Peace be unto you]," a voice greeted her. Immediately she knew who it was. She gave a formal Arabic response, then called out, "Papa!" Silence. "Papa!"

"Yes, it's me. Where are you?"

"I'm in Pune, where I told you I would be."

"OK," he replied. "The day after tomorrow I'll be there." That's all he said.

"Sure. I will wait for you!" she replied.

At the appointed time Yasmin went to the train station to wait for her father's arrival. When he met her, he was very formal. No warm greeting. No smiles. "I was just passing through, and I wanted to see where you are staying," he said. He thought that perhaps she was wasting her life. Her father stayed for two days, talked to all her teachers, and then left. Although he refused to stay on campus and didn't say anything personal to her—not a word—he did leave a suitcase with some clothes and food her mother sent for her. It was the first package Yasmin had received from her parents since they had expelled her from her home two years earlier. Then her father departed for home.

A Second Visit

During the following months her parents telephoned occasionally. Then, during her third year, she received another phone call from her father to tell her he was passing through Pune again and wanted to visit her. This time he asked her to book a guest room at the college. Extremely happy, she gave thanks to God: "O Lord, I know You are working. I can see it!"

On this visit her father was much more friendly. He took her shopping. Since he was staying over a weekend, Yasmin gathered her courage and asked him if he would like to attend church with her. After a silence that seemed like an eternity, he said, "OK." Almost three years earlier she had risked being killed for becoming a Christian, and now her Muslim father was willing to sit next to her in a Christian church. She could feel the gap between them being slowly bridged. God was working.

Yasmin's father spent about a week with her, and then announced, "I have to go home now to care for the family business." She accompanied him to the train station. In Indian culture, if you greet someone in authority, such as your father, you bend down and touch his feet and then touch your head. It is a way of showing respect. So as her father was about to leave the train station, Yasmin bent down and touched his feet. Then when she started to get up to touch her head, her father embraced her! That was the first time in the 22 years of her life that he had actually hugged her. Tears filled his eyes. "Stay well," he said. "I'm happy to see you." Yasmin looked back at her father with tears in her own eyes. Her prayers in Jesus' name were being answered.

Now she goes home every year to see her parents. When they eat together, her father says his prayer in Arabic and then waits for Yasmin to say her prayer of thanks in the name of Jesus. She prays out loud, and her father waits respectfully before they eat together. That is a miracle! Although he had once banished her from his house, he has now come to respect her. While he doesn't know Jesus personally yet, he recognizes through his daughter's life that Jesus is real. And he sees the peace of God in her life.

Pray for Me

Recently Yasmin's father faced some health challenges. "Your father is really in pain," her mother said over the phone, "and he wants to speak to you." Then she heard her father's voice: "I want you to do one thing for me. Will you do it? Will you pray for me?" It was another miracle. Her Muslim father had asked her to pray for him in the name of Jesus. God is still working. Yasmin doesn't know what the future holds, but she realizes that the Lord is in control. She is certain that every prayer offered in the name of Jesus is heard and answered according to God's will. Yasmin has seen evidence time and time again that Jesus is real. And she has noticed His leading every step of her journey.

The Journey Continues

Eleven years after her first lonely train ride from Kolkata to Pune, India, Yasmin is the chair of the Department of Psychology, Guidance, and Counseling at a Christian university in Zambia. God is using her to bless the lives of thousands of students. She is willing to follow wherever He leads, and do whatever He asks her to do. Her life and testimony provide radical evidence that Jesus is more than a great teacher, more than another holy prophet. Jesus is the true Messiah, the Son of God, and the living Lord.

---

[1] Ramadan is the ninth month of the Islamic calendar, when Muslims observe strict fasting from sunrise to sunset.

[2] Jesus gave His disciples instruction on how to pray. Matthew records His teaching, including a model for prayer often referred to as the Lord's Prayer (Matthew 6:6-13).

[3] *Kafir* is an Arabic word used in an Islamic doctrinal sense, translated as "unbeliever," or "infidel." The word refers to a person who rejects God or who hides, denies, or covers the truth of Islam.

2

The Testimony of Paul Ratsara

An Ancestor Worshipper From Rural Madagascar

Paul should have died when he was 16 years old. The poison secretly slipped into his food was slowly killing him. The medicine man could not help him. A one-month stay in the hospital failed to save him, and the doctors sent this firstborn son of a local Malagasy chief home to die. Reduced to skin and bones, Paul awaited his certain fate. Totally unaware of the power of the living God, Paul had been raised in the midst of darkness. Spiritist practices and idols could not protect him from an enemy who wanted him dead.

Rescued From Death

What impressed a former farm employee to return to

the Ratsara farm? How did he know the antidote to the poison? Those vital questions remained unanswered for several months. But the mixture prepared by the returning worker spared Paul's life. After five months of struggle between life and death, he felt new strength begin to surge through his body, but it was just a foretaste of his resurrection life.

Paul had excelled at his local school and had earned a reputation as a rising academic star. Apparently a jealous relative had attempted to kill him, so his mother was afraid to send him back to school. Surely his enemy would try again, and perhaps be successful. No matter how much Paul begged to return to school, his mother's answer was always the same. It seemed he would be a cattle herder for the rest of his days, confined to a life of manual labor on the family farm.

A Book From Heaven

Then everything began to change. Paul found a small book in his house—a Malagasy translation of the New Testament and Psalms. Though he never discovered how it got there, he accepted it as a gift from heaven. Since he was an avid reader and his family owned very few books, he took this volume with him out to the fields. Sitting under the blue Madagascar sky, he began to read the inspired text, starting with the book of Matthew. Like the psalmist David, Paul held communion with heaven in the midst of God's creation. He read the story of the Wise Men who came and worshiped Jesus. Paul learned of sick people healed and demoniacs set free. The teachings of Jesus in the Sermon on the Mount captivated him and His parables about sowers, merchants, and lost sheep fascinated him. When he reached the last three chapters of that first Gospel, Paul's heart began to burn within him. He marveled at the love of Jesus, who gave His life to save us from our sins. The response of his young heart was spontaneous and strong: "I love that Man."

Day by day Paul took this inspired treasure with him into the fields. After inspecting the cattle, he would then read some more from the Holy Scriptures. He journeyed through the entire New Testament and the Psalms. Then he began to go through them a second time, like a hungry man searching for bread. "Blessed are those who hunger and thirst for righteousness, for they will be filled," he read. The promise of Jesus was true. It was being fulfilled in his own life!

Saved for a Purpose

Paul reflected back over his 16 years. Several times his life had been spared. On one occasion he had been caring for his family's cattle when an irritable bull attacked him. Fortunately, Paul was a slender 12-year-old, and the bull's horns slipped around either side of his narrow waist. Thrown to the ground, he looked in horror as the angry bull charged, ready to trample him to death. Who gave Paul the wisdom to scramble under a small bush nearby?

Another time he had tumbled headfirst from the high

branches of a tree. Just before he struck the ground, his arms grasped a branch, and he survived the near-fatal fall with only scrapes and bruises. Surely he was being protected for a reason.

Searching the Scriptures

With an insatiable thirst for learning, Paul longed to go back to school again. Deep in his heart, he sensed that God had a great plan for his life. As a result of much pleading, Paul's mother gave her permission for her son to continue his education. After some months at their local school, he moved to a larger town to finish high school. There he lived with his cousin and her husband. In their home he discovered another treasure—a copy of the entire Bible! To his delight, he could now also read the testimony of Moses and the prophets. Jesus had declared, "These are they that testify of Me" (John 5:39, NKJV). Paul had read the story of Jesus and the disciples on the road to Emmaus, how beginning with Moses and all the prophets He had explained everything in the Scriptures concerning Himself. Now Paul was able to read the Scriptures for himself. He discovered the truth of the psalmist's promise: "Your word is a lamp to my feet and a light to my path" (Psalm 119:105, NKJV).

Sensing a Call to Service

Paul began to attend a Christian church with his cousin

and her husband. Before long he was serving as a youth leader and then a regional leader of Christian young people. One day—a day that he will always remember—Paul heard the clear call of God to become a preacher. It wasn't an audible voice, but rather a firm conviction in his heart and mind. He also received a distinct impression: "Now that you are going to dedicate your entire life to preach the gospel, make sure you preach the truth, not error." As he continued to study the Bible carefully, God led him to some important convictions regarding Bible truth. But he struggled with the divine summons to serve as a pastor. His parents were already disappointed that he had become a Christian. They had high hopes for him to get a high-paying job. Preachers were poor. What was Paul supposed to do?

Deciding to please his parents, he resisted the conviction to become a pastor. He sat for a government exam that would enable him to receive a full scholarship to study engineering at a fine university in the second-largest city in Madagascar. About 1,200 students competed for 12 places. If he was successful, his path to success was assured. Can you guess what happened? Yes, Paul earned one of those 12 scholarships. Soon he was traveling many miles from his home to begin his new adventure, an opportunity of a lifetime—but he was miserable and couldn't concentrate on his studies. After about a month in the program he went to one of the school administrators and announced his intention to return home.

"Are you out of your mind?" the official demanded. Thousands would gladly take his place. But Paul had read the words of Jesus: "No one who puts a hand to the plow and looks back is fit for service in the kingdom of God" (Luke 9:62). When Jesus called His first disciples to follow Him, "they pulled their boats up on shore, left everything and followed him" (Luke 5:11). It was true that he would make lots of money as an engineer, but that was not what God had in mind for his life. Paul didn't want to be like the rich fool in the parable of Jesus who stored up treasure on earth but was not rich toward God (Luke 12:16-21). He remembered the words of Jesus: "What good will it be for someone to gain the whole world, yet forfeit their soul? Or what can anyone give in exchange for their soul?" (Matthew 16:26).

Disowned by His Family

When Paul returned home and announced to his family that he planned to study to become a pastor, his mother stood by the front door of their house and said, "If you walk out of this door, you are no longer my son." Their family was close-knit and filled with love. How could he bear the pain of complete rejection? But then how could he resist the unmistakable call of God? Finally his decision was settled. He ought to obey God rather than any human being. Paul took his suitcase and didn't look back.

After a year of studies to become a pastor, he decided to

return home. Paul missed his family and loved his parents dearly, but would they receive him or reject him once again? When he finally arrived at his home, his parents greeted him with joy. They had missed him too. To his surprise, his father apologized for overreacting and now encouraged him in his classwork as a pastor, even asking his son to study the Bible with them. Day after day Paul opened the Scriptures to his family. He prayed to God that the miracle he had experienced would happen in their lives as well—that their hearts would burn within them as they saw the truth about Jesus in the Holy Scriptures.

Delivered From Death Again

Paul has devoted the rest of his life to sharing Jesus with others. For several years he and his family served in the war-torn country of Zaire (now the Democratic Republic of Congo). "If the soldiers of President Mobutu saw you carrying a bag or case," Paul told me when sharing his testimony, "they would stop you and say, 'Maybe you have a dangerous weapon there. Let me see.' Then they would take everything and warn, 'Don't turn back. Just go.' And you didn't turn back, or they might kill you."

On one occasion bandits kidnapped Paul. As he crossed a main road in Kinshasa, a stranger pulled a gun and pointed it directly at him. Paul remembered the fate of a fellow pastor who had resisted three days earlier when some bandits tried to rob him. They had shot his colleague three times. What was he to do? The bandit pointed toward the open door of a car and demanded that Paul get inside the vehicle. As he sat in the back of that car between two armed gunmen, they demanded that he hand over his papers and wallet. Then they told him they would drive to a quiet place on the banks of the Congo River, kill him, and dump his body in the river. His wife and three children would never know what happened to him. Paul had read the words of the Lord recorded by the psalmist Asaph: "Call on me in the day of trouble; I will deliver you, and you will honor me" (Psalm 50:15). Now it was time to claim that promise. In silent prayer he cried out to God, *Lord, I know if You tarry in Your return to earth, I will eventually die, but this is not the kind of death I wish. Please rescue me!*

In the midst of that crisis Paul felt himself filled with a deep and abiding peace. Jesus announced in the Gospel of John: "Peace I leave with you; my peace I give you. I do not give to you as the world gives. Do not let your hearts be troubled and do not be afraid" (John 14:27). Paul had first read that promise while watching his father's cattle, but now, as he sat sandwiched between two bandits, it was time to experience that supernatural peace again. "I felt Jesus right there by my side," he testified later. "I prayed to Him, 'If You want me to die, I am in Your hands.' I was not afraid." Then Paul turned to the gunmen and said, "I am a missionary from Madagascar. I have come here to serve God and humanity, including you." The bandits didn't want to listen. Suddenly the car began to slow down in a deserted area on the outskirts of town, near the banks of the Congo River. The men began arguing with each other in their own dialect. Finally their chief spoke in French, a language Paul could understand: "No! We aren't going to take this man. He is a man of God. Let him go. We aren't going to keep him." Then the bandit leader turned to Paul and said, "Pastor, we are releasing you. You can go."

Perhaps you are thinking, *That's amazing! Did Paul get out of the car and run for his life?* No. What happened next might surprise you. The prophet Isaiah had declared, "You will keep in perfect peace those whose minds are steadfast, because they trust in you" (Isaiah 26:3). Paul was experiencing God's peace. He remembered the words of the apostle Paul to Christians in Philippi, "Do not be anxious about anything, but in every situation, by prayer and petition, with thanksgiving, present your requests to God. And the peace of God, which transcends all understanding, will guard your hearts and your minds in Christ Jesus" (Philippians 4:6, 7). So instead of running away filled with fear, Paul turned to the bandit chief and said, "Can you give me a ride back?" Foolish? Reckless? Or was his boldness compelling evidence that Jesus is real, a Provider of perfect peace, the true Messiah?

The bandits continued to argue as they drove back to the outskirts of town. Several of them didn't want to return Paul's wallet and travel papers, but the chief insisted. As Paul got out of the car, the leader said, "OK, now we are friends."

"Yes, we are friends. Thank you and God bless you." As Paul turned to leave, the leader pointed in a certain direction: "Go on this road rather than that road, because there might be more bandits on that road." Isn't God amazing? He can even speak words of counsel through a bandit chief.

What did Paul Ratsara discover through that experience? Here is his radical testimony as a devoted follower of Jesus: "I especially like the words of the apostle Paul: 'I consider my life worth nothing to me; my only aim is to finish the race and complete the task the Lord Jesus has given me—the task of testifying to the good news of God's grace' [Acts 20:24]. I have learned that in order to live, you have to be ready to die. In order to be free, you have to be free from the fear of death. When you no longer hold your life dear, you are free. My prayer every day is to be in tune with God every moment, to know that the angels are with me."

God longs to give you peace today. He wants you to experience freedom from anxiety and fear. Just as God spared Paul's life for a reason, your own life has meaning and purpose. God loves you, and He has a wonderful plan for your future. The Lord seeks for you to know Him and Jesus Christ whom He has sent (John 17:3). That is the way to eternal life, eternal peace, and eternal joy.

3

The Testimony of Cleopas

A Disciple of Jesus

Only Luke records the story—not a word from the Gospel writers Matthew, Mark, or John. And at first reading, the narrative leaves us with more questions than answers.

The Emmaus Road

"Now that same day two of them were going to a village called Emmaus, about seven miles from Jerusalem. They were talking with each other about everything that had happened. As they talked and discussed these things with each other, Jesus himself came up and walked along with them; but they were kept from recognizing him.

"He asked them, 'What are you discussing together as you walk along?'

"They stood still, their faces downcast. One of them, named Cleopas, asked him, 'Are you the only one visiting Jerusalem who does not know the things that have happened there in these days?'

" 'What things?' he asked.

" 'About Jesus of Nazareth,' they replied. 'He was a prophet, powerful in word and deed before God and all the people. The chief priests and our rulers handed him over to be sentenced to death, and they crucified him; but we had hoped that he was the one who was going to redeem Israel. And what is more, it is the third day since all this took place. In addition, some of our women amazed us. They went to the tomb early this morning but didn't find his body. They came and told us that they had seen a vision of angels, who said he was alive. Then some of our companions went to the tomb and found it just as the women had said, but they did not see Jesus.'

"He said to them, 'How foolish you are, and how slow of heart to believe all that the prophets have spoken! Did not the Messiah have to suffer these things and then enter his glory?' And beginning with Moses and all the Prophets, he explained to them what was said in all the Scriptures concerning himself.

"As they approached the village to which they were going, Jesus continued on as if he were going farther. But they urged him strongly, 'Stay with us, for it is nearly evening; the day is almost over.' So he went in to stay with them.

"When he was at the table with them, he took bread, gave thanks, broke it and began to give it to them. Then their eyes were opened and they recognized him, and he disappeared from their sight. They asked each other, 'Were not our hearts burning within us while he talked with us on the road and opened the Scriptures to us?'" (Luke 24:13-32).

What "same day" does Luke refer to? We find the answer at the beginning of Luke 24. "On the first day of the week, very early in the morning, the women took the spices they had prepared and went to the tomb" (verse 1). It was the day that Christians call "Easter Sunday." Jesus was crucified on Friday, rested in the tomb on the Sabbath day, and on the first day of the week women came to the tomb and discovered the stone that had sealed it now rolled away. Two angels shared this glorious news: "Why do you look for the living among the dead? He is not here; he has risen!" (verses 5, 6).

It is "that same day," according to Luke, that "two of them" were going to a village called Emmaus. Who were they? According to Luke 24:9 the women who heard the testimony from the angels reported it "to the Eleven and to all the others." The close disciples of Jesus had been referred to as "the Twelve," but then Judas had denied Jesus and betrayed Him with a kiss. Simon Peter also denied Jesus and betrayed Him with a curse, but he repented with tears. Judas, on the other hand, experienced only remorse and subsequently hanged himself. So now it was just the Eleven, rather than the Twelve, but Jesus had many more disciples. Luke records, at the beginning of the book of Acts, that there were about 120 disciples of Jesus gathered for prayer (Acts 1:15). The women gave their testimony about Jesus being raised from the dead not only to the eleven, but also "to all the others" (Luke 24:9).

The Identity of the Two Disciples

The disciples on the road to Emmaus were "two of them." We find one of them named in Luke 24:18 as Cleopas. Who was Cleopas? Some have wondered if he is the same as the Clopas mentioned by the apostle John: "Near the cross of Jesus stood his mother, his mother's sister, Mary the wife of Clopas, and Mary Magdalene" (John 19:25). If Cleopas and Clopas are one and the same, then Cleopas' wife was one of the women who followed Jesus. She was present at the cross with Mary, the mother of Jesus, with Mary's sister, and with Mary Magdalene. She may also have been among, the group of women at the tomb who heard the glorious report from the angels, "He is not here; He has risen!" (Luke 24:6).

A comment Cleopas made to Jesus on the Emmaus road seems to support such a conclusion: "Some of our women amazed us. They went to the tomb early this morning but didn't find his body. They came and told us that they had seen a vision of angels, who said he was alive" (verse 22). But as we'll discover from the next part of the story, Cleopas was skeptical about the report.

What about the other disciple? Some have suggested it was Matthias, who would later become the replacement for Judas, one of the Twelve. Dr. Luke doesn't tell us, but he does offer one interesting piece of information.

The two disciples urge Jesus, "Stay with us, for it is nearly evening; the day is almost over" (verse 29). What can we learn from that comment? Maybe the two disciples were related. That's certainly possible—brothers such as Peter and Andrew, or James and John. Or perhaps it was Cleopas and his son, or Cleopas and his wife. Whoever they were, the two disciples shared the same house, and they invited Jesus to remain with them.

The Village of Emmaus

What have we learned so far? We don't know very much about the two individuals. Cleopas could be Clopas, but we're not sure. And we cannot be certain about the identity of the other disciple. What about Emmaus? Where is that located? Unfortunately, we don't know that, either!

Emmaus was not a city with walls, such as Jerusalem. A walled city was called a *polis,* from which we get the English word "metropolis," but Luke refers to Emmaus as a *kōmē,* a village or country town, as opposed to a walled city. Only here do we find any mention in Scripture of Emmaus. Archaeologists are not sure of its location, though the text tells us it was about 60 stadia from Jerusalem. A stadion was about 185 meters, or 607 feet. So 60 stadia is about 11 kilometers, or a little under seven miles, if you're traveling in a straight line—probably a little longer on a winding road. That distance is important for us, because it gives us some indication of how long the disciples traveled that road. It also gives us a clue as to when they began their journey.

The Walk to Emmaus

How long would it take to walk 11 kilometers, or seven miles? About two to three hours at a normal walking speed. But probably the journey to Emmaus was slower. The two disciples talked together as they headed toward Emmaus, and their conversation became even more intense after they met the stranger along the way. Luke tells us that when they arrived at Emmaus, it was already dusk. The sun sets in that region about 6:30 in the evening, so we can infer that the two disciples left Jerusalem in the early afternoon. They had already received a report from "their women" earlier in the day, and now they returned to their small village of Emmaus. Apparently they had not yet heard the testimony of Mary Magdalene who met with Jesus near the garden tomb.

Discouraged Disciples

So the two disciples were walking home on the road to Emmaus, discussing the events of the past few days. Their Master, Jesus, had been arrested in the Garden of Gethsemane. Next came a mockery of a trial. Even the Roman procurator, Pontius Pilate, had declared Jesus was innocent, but the religious leaders had demanded His death. Then there was the spitting, the beating, and that dreadful flogging. How could God allow the Messiah to receive such treatment? And finally the crucifixion—suspended naked between heaven and earth. Didn't the Scriptures declare, "Cursed is everyone who is hung on a pole?" (Deuteronomy 21:23; Galatians 3:13)? How could such things have happened to the Messiah? Or, worse yet, perhaps Jesus wasn't the Messiah after all.

Cleopas and his companion struggled to make sense of things. The women who went to the tomb where Jesus had been placed had already told them their experience. Apparently two angels had announced to the women, "Why do you look for the living among the dead? He is not here; he has risen!" (Luke 24:5, 6). But the two disciples on the road to Emmaus were obviously still dealing with disappointment, discouragement, and doubt.

The Stranger on the Road

As they discussed these things with each other, Jesus, the risen Lord, caught up with them. It's interesting to note that Luke records that "Jesus Himself drew near" (verse 15, NKJV). It was no hallucination or impersonator, but Jesus risen from the dead. But "they were kept from recognizing him" (verse 16). What does that mean? Did Jesus look different after His resurrection? I don't think so. Other disciples instantly perceived who He was. So what is going on here? Was Jesus wearing a hooded himation and hiding His face, or was something supernatural happening? Be attentive to the rest of the story, and you'll understand the reason for keeping them from recognizing Jesus at first.

Jesus Joins the Conversation

Jesus asked them, "What are you discussing together as you walk along?" (verse 17).

Luke records their initial response: "They stood still, their faces downcast" (verse 17). We get the impression they were almost speechless. Shocked. Perhaps they were thinking to themselves, *Where have you been?* Then Cleopas verbalized his thoughts. "Are you the only one visiting Jerusalem who does not know the things that have happened there in these days?" (verse 18).

Perhaps you can imagine a little amazement in his voice. But Jesus coached Cleopas to share his thoughts.

"What things?" Jesus asked.

"About Jesus of Nazareth," they replied. Now the second disciple was also engaged in the conversation. "He was a prophet, powerful in word and deed before God and all the people. The chief priests and our rulers handed him over to be sentenced to death, and they crucified him; but we had hoped that he was the one who was going to redeem Israel. And what is more, it is the third day since all this took place. In addition, some of our women amazed us. They went to the tomb early this morning but didn't find his body. They came and told us that they had seen a vision of angels, who said he was alive.

Then some of our companions went to the tomb and found it just as the women had said, but they did not see Jesus" (verses 19-24).

What do you hear in their testimony? Disappointment? Discouragement? Doubt? They described Jesus as "a prophet, powerful in word and deed," but they did not call Him Messiah. And they didn't say, "The women saw angels, who said Jesus was alive," but rather "They came and told us that they had seen *a vision of* angels, who said he was alive." Do you see the difference? Cleopas and the unnamed disciple were not walking along the road to Emmaus rejoicing that Jesus was the Messiah and had risen from the dead. They were disappointed, discouraged, and doubting.

How did Jesus respond? "He said to them, 'How foolish you are, and how slow of heart to believe all that the prophets have spoken! Did not the Messiah have to suffer these things and then enter his glory?'" (verses 25, 26).

Why didn't Jesus just announce, "It's Me! Jesus! I have risen from the dead!"? Perhaps for the same reason the disciples were kept from recognizing Him at first. He had something vital to share with them. What would have happened if Jesus had boldly introduced Himself? Those two disciples would have been so excited that they wouldn't have heard anything else.

The Most Important Bible Study Ever Given

But Jesus was about to present the most important Bible

study ever given: "And beginning with Moses and all the Prophets, he explained to them what was said in all the Scriptures concerning himself" (verse 27).

Don't you wish you could have been there to listen as Jesus explained to them what all Scriptures had to say about Himself?

What was the reaction of the two disciples? They asked each other, "Were not our hearts burning within us while he talked with us on the road and opened the Scriptures to us?" (verse 32). What does that mean? They sensed they were uncovering sacred treasure, walking on holy ground.

Before Jesus met with them on the road and showed them all the evidence in the Scriptures concerning Himself, their faith in Him as Messiah had been growing dim. Now their hearts burned within them! That's my prayer for you as we examine the radical evidence from the Scriptures that point to Jesus as the Messiah. I'm praying that your heart will also burn within you as you discover the truths of God's Word that clearly point to Jesus as the Messiah, the Savior of the world!

Their Eyes Were Opened

Did the two disciples on the Emmaus road ever recognize it was Jesus who was speaking to them? Yes! "As they approached the village to which they were going, Jesus continued on as if he were going farther. But they urged him strongly, 'Stay with us, for it is nearly evening; the day is almost over.' So he went in to stay with them. When he was at the table with them, he took bread, gave thanks, broke it and began to give it to them. Then their eyes were opened and they recognized him, and he disappeared from their sight" (verses 28-31).

At last they perceived His identity! Was it the way He broke the bread? Did they see the nailprints in His hands? Or was it now God's appointed time for the veil to be lifted? Luke doesn't give us that information. But this much is certain: when Jesus took the bread, gave thanks, broke it, and gave it to them, they realized who He was!

Then something else supernatural happened: Jesus disappeared from their sight. They would see Him again in the company of the other disciples after they hurried all the way back to Jerusalem, this time in the dark. That's a combined distance back and forth of almost two more than half a marathon, but they were excited! Luke records that when they found where the Eleven were assembled, "the two told what had happened on the way, and how Jesus was recognized by them when he broke the bread" (verse 35).

Jesus Visits the Upper Room

While the two transformed disciples were giving their compelling testimony to the others, "Jesus himself stood among them and said to them, 'Peace be with you.' They were startled and frightened, thinking they saw a ghost. He said to them, 'Why are you troubled, and why do doubts rise in your minds? Look at my hands and my feet. It is I myself! Touch me and see;

a ghost does not have flesh and bones, as you see I have.' When he had said this, he showed them his hands and feet. And while they still did not believe it because of joy and amazement, he asked them, 'Do you have anything here to eat?' They gave him a piece of broiled fish, and he took it and ate it in their presence. He said to them, 'This is what I told you while I was still with you: Everything must be fulfilled that is written about me in the Law of Moses, the Prophets and the Psalms.' Then he opened their minds so they could understand the Scriptures" (verses 36-45).

Jesus Brings Joy

After the larger group of disciples listened to this radical evidence about Jesus, "they worshiped him and returned to Jerusalem with great joy. And they stayed continually at the temple, praising God" (verses 52, 53).

It is a joyful experience when a person perceives Jesus for who He really is—not just another great teacher or even a prophet, powerful in word and deed, but as Messiah, Savior. And not just Savior of the world, but your personal Savior. Cleopas and the other disciples experienced that joy when they recognized Jesus as their Messiah and risen Lord.

People still experience joy today when they examine the compelling evidence from Scripture and come under the conviction of the Holy Spirit that Jesus is the Son of God, the Savior of the world.

David's Testimony

David has a joyful testimony to share. I received his e-mail while I was writing this chapter on the testimony of Cleopas. Born in Hawaii, David now lives in southern California. Recently he read the Bible from cover to cover for the first time. As he went through the stories about Jesus in the New Testament, he found himself with tears running down his face more often than he would ever care to admit. What was happening to him? His heart was burning within him. He was under the conviction of the Holy Spirit, walking on holy ground. The Gospel written by the apostle John especially moved him. "I don't know if the impact this Gospel has had on me is common," David testified, "but this is a very powerful book!"

If the beloved apostle could have seen David reading his Gospel, he would have smiled. John wrote for people just like David, those seeking to know the truth about Jesus. The apostle gave this testimony at the conclusion of his book: "Jesus performed many other signs in the presence of his disciples, which are not recorded in this book. But these are written that you may believe that Jesus is the Messiah, the Son of God, and that by believing you may have life in his name" (John 20:30, 31).

It was obvious to David that he needed help in understanding what he had just read, and he was not sure where to turn. So he asked God if He would lead him to a television program that could provide him the help he was seeking. Is God able to do that? He has promised in Scripture: "I will instruct you and teach you in the way you should go; I will counsel you with my loving eye on you" (Psalm 32:8).

"God must have heard me," David exclaimed, "because the next thing I knew I was watching Hope Sabbath School on DirecTV, channel 368."[1] Hope Sabbath School is an in-depth interactive Bible study broadcast worldwide on the Hope Channel Network. It consists of 12 young adults seeking to know the truth about Jesus and His Word, just like the two disciples on the Emmaus road. Overjoyed at finding the program, David said, "It is fantastic, and I'm learning more and more about the love and grace of God and Jesus Christ."

Recently he heard the Hope Sabbath School team sing the Scripture song "I Have Been Crucified With Christ."[2] Again his heart burned within him and his eyes filled with tears, knowing that Christ gave His life for him and loved him so much.

That miracle of transformation is repeated again and again. God promised through the prophet Jeremiah, "You will seek me and find me when you seek me with all your heart" (Jeremiah 29:13). As you continue prayerfully to examine the compelling evidence from the Bible that points to Jesus as the Messiah, your life will also be changed. Like the first disciples, you too will worship and go out with great joy to share the good news you have learned.

¹ Hope Sabbath School is an in-depth interactive Bible study. To learn more, go to www.hopetv.org/hopess.

² "I Have Been Crucified With Christ" is a TRILOGY Scripture song with lyrics from Galatians 2:20, 21. You can download a copy of this song at iTunes or visit www.trilogyscripturesongs.com.

4

The Testimony of Moses

"And beginning with Moses . . . he explained to them what was said in all the Scriptures concerning himself" (Luke 24:27). I used to wish someone had recorded that Bible study, but now I'm convinced Jesus wants us to search the Scriptures for ourselves. We need to reconstruct that in-depth Bible study so that our hearts can also burn within us as we examine the radical evidence concerning Jesus as Messiah.

Beginning With Moses

Why do you think Jesus began His amazing Bible study with the testimony of Moses? The Old Testament has more than 1,000 prophecies and types that find their fulfillment in Jesus of Nazareth.[1] Most of those prophecies are not in the books of Moses.[2] So why did Jesus start with the testimony of Moses? Let me suggest two possible reasons. The first is that the Hebrew Scriptures begin with the books of Moses. During the time of Jesus, the Jews divided what we today call the Old Testament into three parts: the books of Moses (also referred to as the Law or the Torah), the Prophets, and the Psalms and Writings. Perhaps Jesus began with the testimony of Moses because it came first in the Hebrew Scriptures.

A second possible reason was that Jesus met the two disciples where they were. Perhaps they were talking about the Mosaic writings, and Jesus started there as He opened the Scriptures to them. That's what happened when Philip the deacon met an Ethiopian official on the road from Jerusalem to Gaza. Dr. Luke records in the book of Acts that the official was traveling in his chariot, reading a prophecy about the Messiah in the book of the prophet Isaiah. When Philip ran up alongside the chariot, the Ethiopian invited him to join him in his study: "The eunuch asked Philip, 'Tell me, please, who is the prophet talking about, himself or someone else?' Then Philip began with that very passage of Scripture and told him the good news about Jesus" (Acts 8:34, 35).

Philip didn't commence with Daniel or Malachi. He connected with the Ethiopian at the point of his need. The court official had a question: "Who is the prophet talking about?" So Philip began with the writings of the prophet Isaiah and shared their compelling evidence regarding Jesus as Messiah. Perhaps the two disciples on the road to Emmaus were discussing the writings of Moses as they walked along, trying to understand the promises regarding the Messiah, and Jesus met them at the point of their need.

The Suffering of Messiah

Whatever the reason, Dr. Luke records that Jesus first focused on the testimony of Moses concerning the Messiah—and not just anything about Messiah, but particularly the issue of whether or not He would have to suffer. "Did not the Messiah have to suffer these things and then enter his glory?" He asked the two disciples (Luke 24:26).

The Jews in the time of Jesus assumed that the Messiah would come as a victorious conqueror. They thought He would throw off the yoke of Rome and restore Israel to its former glory. That's why these two disciples on the road to Emmaus now struggled to understand what had just happened to Jesus. The Romans had beaten, mocked, flogged, and killed Him. That's not the kind of treatment they had expected the Messiah to receive.

So where would Jesus have started in the writings of Moses? I imagine He might have commenced with the words of hope recorded in Genesis 3:15. Our first parents had both sinned against God. Eve listened to the seductive lie of the serpent, and Adam had willfully joined her in rebellion against God. But God did not abandon them. Speaking in their presence, He said to the serpent, "I will put enmity between you and the woman, and between your offspring and hers; he will crush your head, and you will strike his heel" (Genesis 3:15).

One of the offspring of the woman would crush the head of the serpent. It is the first mention of the coming of a deliverer or redeemer. Notice that the seed would be part of the human family. The apostle Paul clearly identifies this Offspring, this Seed of the woman, as Jesus Christ (Galatians 3:16). He would crush the serpent's head—that old serpent, the devil or Satan, as the apostle John calls him in Revelation 12:9. But the serpent would also strike the Redeemer's heel. The Messiah would suffer. "Did not the Messiah have to suffer these things and then enter his glory?"

The Lord Will Provide

I imagine Jesus reminded the two disciples of the story of the great patriarch Abraham and his son Isaac, also recorded by Moses in the book of Genesis. Isaac was a miracle child—a child of promise. Abram's wife, Sarai, was barren, but God promised Abram that his descendants would be as numerous as the stars of heaven. And the Lord God was faithful to His promise. Sarai conceived and bore a son. Isaac was a fulfillment of divine promise.

Then the story found in the book of Genesis takes an unexpected twist: "Some time later God tested Abraham. He said to him, 'Abraham!'

"'Here I am,' he replied.

"Then God said, 'Take your son, your only son, whom you love—Isaac—and go to the region of Moriah. Sacrifice him there as a burnt offering on a mountain I will show you.'

"Early the next morning Abraham got up and loaded his donkey. He took with him two of his servants and his son Isaac. When he had cut enough wood for the burnt offering, he set out for the place God had told him about.

"On the third day Abraham looked up and saw the place in the distance. He said to his servants, 'Stay here with the donkey while I and the boy go over there. We will worship and then we will come back to you.'

"Abraham took the wood for the burnt offering and placed it on his son Isaac, and he himself carried the fire and the knife. As the two of them went on together, Isaac spoke up and said to his father Abraham, 'Father?'

"'Yes, my son?' Abraham replied.

"'The fire and wood are here,' Isaac said, 'but where is the lamb for the burnt offering?'

"Abraham answered, 'God himself will provide the lamb for the burnt offering, my son.' And the two of them went on together.

"When they reached the place God had told him about, Abraham built an altar there and arranged the wood on it. He bound his son Isaac and laid him on the altar, on top of the wood. Then he reached out his hand and took the knife to slay his son.

But the angel of the Lord called out to him from heaven, 'Abraham! Abraham!'

" 'Here I am,' he replied.

" 'Do not lay a hand on the boy,' he said. 'Do not do anything to him. Now I know that you fear God, because you have not withheld from me your son, your only son.'

"Abraham looked up and there in a thicket he saw a ram caught by its horns. He went over and took the ram and sacrificed it as a burnt offering instead of his son. So Abraham called that place The Lord Will Provide. And to this day it is said, 'On the mountain of the Lord it will be provided' " (Genesis 22:1-14).

YHWH Yireh. Jehovah Jireh. "The Lord will provide." Perhaps Abraham thought his own son Isaac was the Redeemer—the Seed of the woman who would crush the serpent's head. Perhaps the miracle child Isaac could be the Messiah. Whatever might have gone through his mind, Abraham simply received God's assurance, "The Lord will provide."

Two thousand years later Jesus testified, "Your father Abraham rejoiced at the thought of seeing my day; he saw it and was glad" (John 8:56). Why was Abraham glad as he looked forward by faith? Because the Lord would provide. And on that same mountain where God spoke to Abraham and Isaac, on that same Mount Moriah more than 2,000 years later, the Lord did exactly that. He fulfilled His promise! Perhaps Jesus reviewed this story with His two disciples on the road to Emmaus.

The Passover Lamb

Surely Jesus would have reminded the two disciples about the first Passover, as the children of Israel prepared to leave Egypt. God directed each family to take the blood of a lamb and put it on the doorpost of their dwelling. You can read the story in Exodus 12. The Lord declared to Moses, "Now the blood shall be a sign for you on the houses where you are. And when I see the blood, I will pass over you" (Exodus 12:13, NKJV).

The death of the lamb didn't accomplish anything in itself. But it was a symbol, pointing forward to the Lamb that God would furnish. Who was that Lamb? John the Baptist declared of Jesus, "Behold! The Lamb of God who takes away the sin of the world!" (John 1:29, NKJV). Had the disciples on the Emmaus road forgotten that the Lamb would be slain? Jesus now reminded them from the testimony of Moses, "Did not the Messiah have to suffer these things and then enter his glory?"

Striking the Rock

I imagine that Jesus also told a story recorded in the second book of Moses, the book of Exodus.

"The whole Israelite community set out from the Desert of Sin, traveling from place to place as the Lord commanded. They camped at Rephidim, but there was no water for the people to drink. So they quarreled with Moses and said, 'Give us water to drink.'

"Moses replied, 'Why do you quarrel with me? Why do you put the Lord to the test?'

"But the people were thirsty for water there, and they grumbled against Moses. They said, 'Why did you bring us up out of Egypt to make us and our children and livestock die of thirst?'

"Then Moses cried out to the Lord, 'What am I to do with these people? They are almost ready to stone me.'

"The Lord answered Moses, 'Go out in front of the people. Take with you some of the elders of Israel and take in your hand the staff with which you struck the Nile, and go. I will stand there before you by the rock at Horeb. Strike the rock, and water will come out of it for the people to drink.' So Moses did this in the sight of the elders of Israel" (Exodus 17:1-6).

Whom did that rock represent? The psalmist declared, "To you I will cry, O Lord my Rock" (Psalm 28:1, NKJV) and "Come, let us sing for joy to the Lord; let us shout aloud to the Rock of our salvation" (Psalm 95:1). Under the inspiration of the Holy Spirit the apostle Paul specifically refers to the rock that Moses struck in the wilderness: "[they] drank the same spiritual drink; for they drank from the spiritual rock that accompanied them, and that rock was Christ" (1 Corinthians 10:4).

So what was the significance of the striking of the rock? Why did God instruct Moses to do so? I imagine Jesus asking the two disciples that question as they walked along the road to Emmaus. When the rock was struck, a stream of life flowed forth. So the Messiah would be stricken, and a stream of eternal life would issue from Him.

But what about entering into His glory? Didn't Jesus say in Luke 24:26, "Did not the Messiah have to suffer these things *and then enter his glory?*" Does Moses testify anywhere about Messiah entering into glory? It's clear from his writings that Messiah would suffer, but what about a glorious ending?

I'm going to give you a homework assignment! Remember, Jesus doesn't offer us the whole Bible study in outline form, because He wants us to search it for ourselves. I encourage you to study the testimony of Moses. Jesus said, "These are they which testify of Me" (John 5:39, NKJV). See if you can find a reference in the testimony of Moses to a glorious ending for Messiah.[3]

The Witness of Job

I will share one testimony of a glorious ending not found in the five best-known books of Moses. It appears in one written even before that of Genesis—a book that many believe Moses authored during his 40-year sojourn in the wilderness of Midian. It's the story of a man of God named Job, who lived in the land of Uz. We could devote an entire chapter to a study of the book of Job, but I want to focus on his words recorded in Job 19:25: "I know that my redeemer lives, and that in the end he will stand on the earth."

According to the testimony of Moses through the book of Job, the story of Messiah doesn't end with sufferings and death. Our Redeemer lives! Did Jesus share those words recorded by Moses with the two disciples on the road to Emmaus? We don't know for sure. But this much we do know—as Jesus opened the Scriptures to them, beginning with the testimony of Moses, and showing them everything concerning Himself, their hearts burned within them. Why? Because it became absolutely clear to them that Jesus was indeed the Messiah. His sufferings and death did not disqualify Him from being the Messiah. Rather, they demonstrated that He was indeed the Messiah.

Prophecy Fulfilled

Before Moses died, he presented a prophecy: "The Lord your God will raise up for you a prophet like me from among you, from your fellow Israelites. You must listen to him" (Deuteronomy 18:15). Who was that prophet? The Jews of Jesus' time were still waiting for that individual. In fact, they asked John the Baptist, "Are you the Prophet?" (John 1:21), referring back to the prophecy of Moses. But John the Baptist said, "I am not." A voice crying in the wilderness, John had come to prepare the way for Jesus Christ, the Word of God made flesh. He was the one of whom Moses testified.

When Jesus gave His Bible study to those two disciples on the road to Emmaus, perhaps they remembered what He had already revealed to them before His sufferings and death. "This is what I told you while I was still with you," Jesus said. "Everything must be fulfilled that is written about me in the Law of Moses, the Prophets and the Psalms" (Luke 24:44).

Jesus had explained that everything written about Him in the Law of Moses, the Prophets, and the Psalms must indeed come to pass. The two disciples should not have been downcast that day. If they had diligently examined the radical evidence in the Scriptures, they would have emerged with the clear conviction that Jesus was indeed the Messiah.

But the disciples had allowed their preconceived ideas to blind their eyes. Jesus had clearly declared, "We are going up to Jerusalem, and the Son of Man will be delivered over to the chief priests and the teachers of the law. They will condemn him to death and will hand him over to the Gentiles, who will mock him and spit on him, flog him and kill him. Three days later he will rise" (Mark 10:33, 34). Why didn't the disciples believe Him? Why weren't they rejoicing all weekend that Jesus would rise on the third day? Why weren't they praising God as they walked on the road to Emmaus?

It's easy to sit in judgment on the disciples, but I have a question for you (and for me as well). Are we diligently searching the Scriptures to learn more about Jesus, our Messiah? Are we setting aside our preconceived ideas and letting God's Word illuminate our minds?

The testimony of Moses clearly points to Jesus as the Messiah, the Savior of the world. And Jesus, your Messiah, your Savior, wants to walk with you. He wants to open your eyes, your understanding. Do you remember the testimony of the two disciples on the Emmaus road? "Were not our hearts burning within us while he talked with us on the road and opened the Scriptures to us?" (Luke 24:32). I'm praying that you will have a similar experience as you search Scripture for yourself.

Evelyne's Testimony

Evelyne began her life in Port-au-Prince, Haiti. Her parents were childhood sweethearts and holocaust survivors. Having escaped from Hitler's rule in Vienna, Austria, in 1938, Fritz and Annie had set sail for South America. Before their ship arrived in Buenos Aires, Argentina had closed its doors to the Jews. They had one last chance to survive—Haiti. God touched the heart of a Haitian resident named Charles Bigio to sponsor the entire ship, or Evelyne's story might have ended at sea, a wishful thought in the minds of her yet-unmarried parents.

Once safely on shore in Haiti, Fritz and Annie were married and established their new home. Two years later Evelyne was born. Her parents raised her in a nominal Jewish home—they celebrated the yearly feasts but did not observe Sabbath. She heard the testimony of Moses but did not comprehend its meaning.

When Evelyne was a teenager, her parents sent her to a Christian boarding school based on the recommendation of a Christian missionary couple that had befriended them. They had no desire for Evelyne to learn about Christianity, but Florida was far away from Haiti, where she was having "boy problems," and Forest Lake Academy was cheaper than a Jewish boarding school. At the Christian boarding school Evelyne learned about her Messiah, Jesus. As she understood more about Jesus, her heart burned within her. Jesus was more than another great teacher, more than another holy prophet. He was the Messiah—her Messiah! Joy and peace flooded her soul.

Evelyne made plans to attend a Christian college, but her hopes shattered when her angry father threatened to disown her if she did not renounce her newfound faith in Jesus. Without direction and hope Evelyne began a downward spiral. Instead of following Jesus no matter what the personal cost, she went searching for meaning in all of the wrong places.

During her third marriage Evelyne got involved with a cult group called I AM. It taught her to believe in Jesus, but not the Messiah she had discovered at the Christian boarding school. According to her cult teachers, Jesus was just one of many spiritual masters. And the Bible? They never read it.

Then one of her former high school classmates told her about an online church service broadcast from the Christian church next to her old boarding school. She started to log on every week and listened to the teachings from Scripture. Her heart began to burn within her once again, and she felt as if she were coming home. After attending church online for several years, Evelyne decided it was time to make a public confession of her faith in Jesus as her Messiah. Having rejected the false teaching that Jesus was just one of many spiritual masters, she was ready to acknowledge Him as the true Messiah—her Messiah.

Evelyne discovered that Jesus doesn't leave you where He finds you. According to her own testimony, she "got a talking-to by God." Startling impressions came to her: "We cannot have you involved in an adulterous relationship and still work for God." "You do not have a broken heart—we are giving you a new heart." "And you do not have to leave the country to work for God." Startled, Evelyne responded in humble obedience: "OK, God." She immediately severed the adulterous relationship and involved herself in a unique Christian ministry, rather than waiting for some special overseas mission adventure. Using her special gift of sewing, Evelyne became an active member of a Prayers and Squares quilting ministry. It has distributed more than 2,000 prayer quilts to families both locally and around the world, reminding hurting individuals and families that someone is praying for them.

Evelyne will always be thankful for those who prayed for her, including the Christian missionaries who befriended her family so many years ago in Haiti. Only in the kingdom of heaven will they see the miracle of transformation that Jesus performed in her life.

---

[1] Liberal scholars reject any prophecies in the Hebrew Scriptures as a direct reference to Jesus and regard them as purely local in their application. For example, they interpret the prophecy of Isaiah 7:14 as relevant only to the prophet's time and place. However, the apostle Matthew would disagree with that conclusion: "All this took place to fulfill what the Lord had said through the prophet: 'The virgin will conceive and give birth to a son, and they will call him Immanuel' (which means 'God with us')" (Matthew 1:22, 23). Matthew recognized Isaiah's messianic prophecy as a reliable testimony of "what the Lord had said through the prophet."

[2] The majority of the messianic prophecies appear in the prophetic writings and the psalms.

[3] You can share with me the results of your study at dmorris@radical evidence.com.

5

The Testimony of the Prophets

What prophecies concerning Messiah from the Hebrew prophets do you think Jesus might have quoted to His two disciples on the road to Emmaus?

The Prophecy of Micah

Perhaps Jesus mentioned a prophecy from Micah: "But you, Bethlehem Ephrathah, though you are small among the clans of Judah, out of you will come for me one who will be ruler over Israel, whose origins are from of old, from ancient times" (Micah 5:2). This prophecy met its fulfillment 700 years later at the birth of Jesus in Bethlehem. Here is the testimony of Luke: "In those days Caesar Augustus issued a decree that a census should be taken of the entire Roman world. (This was the first census that took place while Quirinius was governor of Syria.) And everyone went to their own town to register. So Joseph also went up from the town of Nazareth in Galilee to Judea, to Bethlehem the town of David, because he belonged to the house and line of David. He went there to register with Mary, who was pledged to be married to him and was expecting a child. While they were there, the time came for the baby to be born, and she gave birth to her firstborn, a son. She wrapped him in cloths and placed him in a manger, because there was no guest room available for them" (Luke 2:1-7). Matthew adds his witness: "After Jesus was born in Bethlehem in Judea, during the time of King Herod, Magi from the east came to Jerusalem and asked, 'Where is the one who has been born king of the Jews? We saw his star in the east and have come to worship him'" (Matthew 2:1, 2).

Jesus didn't choose where He would be born! His mother, Mary, lived in Nazareth, where her husband, Joseph, worked as a carpenter (Matthew 13:55). But at the right time, in the right place, a prophecy concerning Messiah came to its completion, and Jesus was born in Bethlehem.

The Prophecy of Zechariah

Another prophecy concerning the Messiah that Jesus may have cited is that of Zechariah: "Rejoice greatly, O daughter of Zion! Shout, O daughter of Jerusalem! Behold, your King is coming to you; He is just and having salvation, lowly and riding on a donkey, a colt, the foal of a donkey" (Zechariah 9:9, NKJV). It saw its fulfillment more than 500 years later in the life of Jesus of Nazareth. Luke records, "After Jesus had said this, he went on ahead, going up to Jerusalem. As he approached Bethphage and Bethany at the hill called the Mount of Olives, he sent two of his disciples, saying to them, 'Go to the village ahead of you, and as you enter it, you will find a colt tied there, which no one has ever ridden. Untie it and bring it here. If anyone asks you, 'Why are you untying it?' tell him, 'The Lord needs it.'"

"Those who were sent ahead went and found it just as he had told them. As they were untying the colt, its owners asked them, 'Why are you untying the colt?'

"They replied, 'The Lord needs it.'

"They brought it to Jesus, threw their cloaks on the colt and put Jesus on it. As he went along, people spread their cloaks on the road. When he came near the place where the road goes down the Mount of Olives, the whole crowd of disciples began joyfully to praise God in loud voices for all the miracles they had seen:

"'Blessed is the king who comes in the name of the Lord!'

"'Peace in heaven and glory in the highest!'

"Some of the Pharisees in the crowd said to Jesus, 'Teacher, rebuke your disciples!'

"'I tell you,' he replied, 'if they keep quiet, the stones will cry out'" (Luke 19:28-40). What Zechariah presented more than 500 years earlier about the Messiah came to pass in every detail in the life of Jesus of Nazareth.

The Prophecy of Malachi

The prophet Malachi declared: "See, I will send my messenger, who will prepare the way before me" (Malachi 3:1). Whom did he refer to? John the Baptist! The prophet Malachi continues: "Then suddenly the Lord you are seeking will come to his temple; the messenger of the covenant, whom you desire, will come, says the Lord Almighty. But who can endure the day of his coming? Who can stand when he appears? For he will be like a refiner's fire or a launderer's soap" (verses 1, 2).

That prophecy had two fulfillments 400 years later in the ministry of Jesus. The apostle John records the first time that Jesus, having begun His ministry as Messiah, entered His Temple: "When it was almost time for the Jewish Passover, Jesus went up to Jerusalem. In the temple courts he found people selling cattle, sheep and doves, and others sitting at tables exchanging money. So he made a whip out of cords, and drove all from the temple courts, both sheep and cattle; he scattered the coins of the money changers and overturned their tables. To those who sold doves he said, 'Get these out of here! Stop turning my Father's house into a market!'" (John 2:13-16).

Why didn't the religious leaders try to stop Him? Malachi had prophesied more than 400 years earlier, "Who can endure the day of his coming? Who can stand when he appears? For he will be like a refiner's fire or a launderer's soap" (Malachi 3:1, 2). And the apostle John recorded that "his disciples remembered that it is written: 'Zeal for your house will consume me.'

"The Jews then responded to him, 'What sign can you show us to prove your authority to do all this?'

"Jesus answered them, 'Destroy this temple, and I will raise it again in three days'" (John 2:17-19).

That was a clear prophecy by Jesus about His death and resurrection. But the religious leaders didn't change their behavior. Many of them probably said to themselves, "We're never going to let Jesus of Nazareth treat us like that again!" But three years later He again came to His Temple, and Matthew records that "Jesus entered the temple courts and drove out all who were buying and selling there. He overturned the tables of the money changers and the benches of those selling doves. 'It is written,' he said to them, '"My house will be called a house of prayer," but you are making it "a den of robbers."' The blind and the lame came to him at the temple, and he healed them. But when the chief priests and the teachers of the law saw the wonderful things he did and the children shouting in the temple courts, 'Hosanna to the Son of David,' they were indignant.

"'Do you hear what these children are saying?' they asked him.

"'Yes,' replied Jesus, 'have you never read, "From the lips of children and infants you, Lord, have called forth your praise"?'" (Matthew 21:12-16).

The Prophecies of Isaiah

I'm certain that in His Bible study on the Emmaus road Jesus mentioned the prophecies of Isaiah. More than 700 years before

Jesus' birth the prophet Isaiah had foretold, "Therefore the Lord himself will give you a sign: The virgin will conceive and give birth to a son, and will call him Immanuel" (Isaiah 7:14). Critics insist that the prophecy has nothing to do with Jesus of Nazareth. But the apostle Matthew would strongly disagree with their assertion: "All this took place to fulfill what the Lord had said through the prophet: 'The virgin will conceive and give birth to a son, and they will call him Immanuel' (which means 'God with us')" (Matthew 1:22, 23). The Gospel writer recognized Isaiah's messianic prophecy as a revelation "the Lord had said" in reference to the coming Messiah, Jesus.

The prophet Isaiah had also foretold that Messiah would take a special interest in Galilee of the Gentiles: "Nevertheless, there will be no more gloom for those who were in distress. In the past he humbled the land of Zebulun and the land of Naphtali, but in the future he will honor Galilee of the nations, by the Way of the Sea, beyond the Jordan—

"The people walking in darkness have seen a great light; on those living in the land of deep darkness a light has dawned" (Isaiah 9:1, 2). Seven hundred years before the ministry of Jesus, Isaiah prophesied that Messiah would show a special concern for Galilee and its people, something totally contrary to traditional expectation. The Galileans were social outcasts, a mixture of ethnic groups imported after the Assyrian invasion of the eighth century B.C. But Luke records that the ministry of Jesus brought the messianic prophecy to pass: "Jesus returned to Galilee in the power of the Spirit, and news about him spread through the whole countryside. He was teaching in their synagogues, and everyone praised him" (Luke 4:14, 15).

But most of all, I'm certain Jesus cited the later prophecies of Isaiah. Remember the words of Jesus recorded in Luke 24:26: "Did not the Messiah have to suffer these things and then enter his glory?" No prophet describes the sufferings of Messiah more vividly than Isaiah. Jesus must have reminded His two disciples of the prophecy recorded in Isaiah 50:6, 7: "I offered my back to those who beat me, my cheeks to those who pulled out my beard; I did not hide my face from mocking and spitting. Because the Sovereign Lord helps me, I will not be disgraced. Therefore have I set my face like flint, and I know I will not be put to shame."

I also hear Jesus quoting from Isaiah 53:

"Who has believed our message and to whom has the arm of the Lord been revealed? He grew up before him like a tender shoot, and like a root out of dry ground. He had no beauty or majesty to attract us to him, nothing in his appearance that we should desire him. He was despised and rejected by mankind, a man of suffering, and familiar with pain. Like one from whom people hide their faces, he was despised, and we held him in low esteem. Surely he took up our pain and bore our suffering, yet we considered him punished by God, stricken by him, and afflicted. But he was pierced for our transgressions, he was crushed for our iniquities; the punishment that brought us peace was on him, and by his wounds we are healed. We all, like sheep, have gone astray, each of us has turned to our own way; and the Lord has laid on him the iniquity of us all. He was oppressed and afflicted, yet he did not open his mouth; he was led like a lamb to the slaughter, and as a sheep before her shearers is silent, so he did not open his mouth. By oppression and judgment he was taken away. Yet who of his generation protested? For he was cut off from the land of the living; for the transgression of my people he was stricken. He was assigned a grave with the wicked, and with the rich in his death, though he had done no violence, nor was any deceit in his mouth. Yet it was the Lord's will to crush him and cause him to suffer, and though the Lord makes his life an offering for sin, he will see his offspring and prolong his days, and the will of the Lord will prosper in his hand. After the suffering of his soul, he will see the light of life and be satisfied; by his knowledge my righteous servant will justify many, and he will bear their iniquities. Therefore I will give him a portion among the great, and he will divide the spoils with the strong, because he poured out his life unto death, and was numbered with the transgressors. For he bore the sin of many, and made intercession for the transgressors" (verses 1-12).

Examine the Evidence

I urge you to read the following chapters from the New Testament: Matthew 26 and 27, Mark 14 and 15, Luke 22 and 23, and John 18 and 19. Every single detail of Isaiah's great messianic prophecy met its completion in the life and death of Jesus of Nazareth.

Examine the evidence. The testimony of the prophets is clear.

Jesus is the Messiah! Hundreds of prophecies concerning the Messiah were fulfilled in every detail in the birth, life, death, and resurrection of Jesus from the dead.

Transformation in Mongolia

As Bold Batsukh examined the evidence of the Scriptures he found himself deeply moved. Despite being indoctrinated with atheistic Communism in Mongolia, Bold had searched for meaning through a study of Tibetan Buddhism. His Buddhist monk taught him that our existence has no purpose. We must try to overcome self and sinful thoughts through meditation, and at the end of our spiritual journey we will suffer based on the amount of sinful acts we have committed. His teacher made no mention of a Creator-God or a Savior. Instead, by his own merit he could become a god. But countless hours of chanting and mystic rituals to unleash and control supernatural powers failed to satisfy the longing of Bold's soul.

His sister was also searching for meaning and hope. She had connected with a young couple in their capital city who were followers of Jesus. The only knowledge Bold had about Jesus had come from reading a schoolbook on history. A section about a person called Jesus described Him as mentally challenged and as someone whose followers betrayed and killed Him after He claimed to be God. Bold wondered why his sister would involve herself with people who believed such strange ideas. "We are Mongolians," he asserted angrily. "We have to respect our own religion and not follow foreign ones."

Bold registered for college as an English major and began his studies. Perhaps mastering English would open a door to a successful and happy life. At first he struggled with his studies and realized that he needed help. Deciding to swallow his pride, he asked his sister if he could accompany her to the meetings she was attending. "I want to learn English, and I need some assistance. Could you ask your teachers if I could come? But I will have nothing to do with their religion, because I'm a devout Buddhist." She said she would inquire. The next day she told Bold that her teachers would be happy to help him.

When he entered their apartment, he saw about a dozen people sitting in a circle and studying the Bible. Bold listened attentively. He found the in-depth Bible study to be a genuine experience of fellowship, of caring for one another, of discussing and sharing ideas and asking questions without any hesitation.

Sometime later someone gave Bold a Bible. When he started reading the testimony of Moses in the book of Genesis, it moved him. The message was so simple and yet so profound: "In the beginning God created the heavens and the earth" (Genesis 1:1). Listen to his own testimony: "The Bible was very clear. God created the world in such an orderly manner. Things didn't just evolve, but were created with love. When it came to the creation of humanity, I was impressed with how God took much care creating us in His image. I was so relieved to find a God who cares. At that moment I found meaning in my life. I was very valuable. I could trust this God who was very orderly, caring, and loving. Since those days my life has never been the same."

Later Bold learned that the loving Creator became flesh and dwelt among us. He read, "In the beginning was the Word, and the Word was with God, and the Word was God. He was in the beginning with God. All things were made through Him, and without Him nothing was made that was made. . . . And the Word became flesh and dwelt among us, and we beheld His glory, the glory as of the only begotten of the Father, full of grace and truth" (John 1:1-14, NKJV). Bold was amazed to discover that hundreds of prophecies about Messiah found their fulfillment in the life of Jesus of Nazareth. After examining the radical evidence, Bold decided to become a devoted follower of Jesus. He is now a transformed witness with his own compelling testimony. He knows deep in his soul that Jesus is more than just another great teacher—He is Immanuel, God with us (see Matthew 1:18-23).

What does such compelling evidence have to do with you today? That same Jesus, that same Messiah, that same Savior who walked with the two disciples on the road to Emmaus and now journeys with Bold in Mongolia, wants to accompany you in your life. He loves you. Caring about you wherever you are on life's road, He will meet you in the midst of your sorrows, your anxieties, your cares, and your joys. He wants to be your Savior and for you to be a part of His kingdom that shall never pass away. Jesus longs for you to experience an intimate encounter with Him, and when that happens, your heart will also burn within you!

6

The Testimony of the Psalmists

My wife and I love to sing scripture songs. We sing when we walk in the mornings, as part of our worship together, and even when traveling in the car. It all started when our children were little. My wife felt impressed to compose scripture songs to help our children memorize the Bible. That was more than 20 years ago. Now our children are grown, but through the years those scripture songs have shaped their lives. In fact, singing scripture songs from God's Word has profoundly affected our whole family. I'm so thankful today for a wonderful Christian wife who has helped us hide God's Word in our hearts!

But scripture songs are not a new idea. Did you realize that the Bible has a whole collection of them? It's called the book of Psalms, although we should probably refer to it as

the *books* of Psalms, because it consists of five collections of
songs all bundled into one. Several psalmists composed them.
The most well known was David, but many others contributed
to the five collections: David's son Solomon, Asaph, the sons of
Korah, and Moses. And the psalms are more than human songs
about God. Here is one psalmist's testimony: "The Spirit of the
Lord spoke through me; his word was on my tongue" (2 Samuel
23:2). God inspired each of the psalmists to give their testimonies in song.

Some of the best known psalms are songs of praise, songs
of worship, of confession and of petition. Most people don't
realize that this collection of scripture songs also contains
more than 90 prophecies about the Messiah.

Having already considered the testimony of Moses and
that of the prophets about the Messiah, perhaps you're wondering, *Why are we now examining the testimony of the
psalmists?* We find the answer to that question in a comment
made by Jesus sometime after His walk on the road to Emmaus. Speaking to a larger group of disciples gathered in a
room in Jerusalem, He said, "Everything must be fulfilled
that is written about me in the Law of Moses, the Prophets
and the Psalms" (Luke 24:44). Jesus then gave a more exten-
sive Bible study than He had to the two disciples. "Then he
opened their minds so they could understand the Scriptures"
(verse 45).

Startling Prophecy About Messiah

In this chapter we will focus primarily on one psalm that had every prophetic detail fulfilled in the life, death, and resurrection of Jesus, thus pointing to Him as the Messiah.

Sufferings and Death

Psalm 22 begins with these startling words: "My God, my God, why have you forsaken me?" (verse 1). I can hear you saying, "Stop right there!" since the Gospel of Mark records those same words. Jesus cried them from the cross (Mark 15:34).

The psalmist continued, under the inspiration of the Spirit of God: "Why are you so far from saving me, so far from my cries of anguish? My God, I cry out by day, but you do not answer, by night, but I find no rest. Yet you are enthroned as the Holy One; you are the one Israel praises. In you our ancestors put their trust; they trusted and you delivered them. To you they cried out and were saved; in you they trusted and were not put to shame. But I am a worm and not a man, scorned by everyone, despised by the people. All who see me mock me; they hurl insults, shaking their heads. 'He trusts in the Lord' they say, 'let the Lord rescue him. Let him deliver him, since he delights in him'" (Psalm 22:1-8).

Didn't the enemies of Jesus mock and insult Him while He hung on the cross? Listen to the testimony of Matthew: "Those who passed by hurled insults at him, shaking their heads and saying, 'You who are going to destroy the temple and build it in three days, save yourself! Come down from the cross, if you are the Son of God!' In the same way the chief priests, the teachers of the law and the elders mocked him. 'He saved others,' they said, 'but he can't save himself! He's the king of Israel! Let him come down now from the cross, and we will believe in him. He trusts in God. Let God rescue him now if he wants him, for he said, 'I am the Son of God'" (Matthew 27:39-43). Psalm 22 prophesied that mockery, those insults, 1,000 years beforehand!

"Yet you brought me out of the womb," the inspired psalmist declared; "you made me trust in you even at my mother's breast. From birth I was cast upon you; from my mother's womb you have been my God. Do not be far from me, for trouble is near and there is no one to help. Many bulls surround me; strong bulls of Bashan encircle me. Roaring lions that tear their prey open their mouths wide against me. I am poured out like water, and all my bones are out of joint" (Psalm 22:9-14).

Notice that the psalmist doesn't say "All my bones are broken" but rather "All of my bones are out of joint." We find this prophecy also fulfilled in the person of Jesus. Although it was customary to break the legs of a crucified criminal, the apostle John declared, "But when they came to Jesus and found that he was already dead, they did not break his legs. Instead, one of the soldiers pierced Jesus' side with a spear, bringing a sudden flow of blood and water. The man who saw it has given testimony, and his testimony is true. He knows that he tells the truth, and he testifies so that you also may believe. These things happened so that the scripture would be fulfilled: 'Not one of his bones will be broken'" (John 19:33-36). Here the apostle John quoted another prophecy given by the psalmist David: "The righteous person may have many troubles, but the Lord delivers him from them all; he protects all his bones, not one of them will be broken" (Psalm 34:19, 20).

"My heart has turned to wax; it has melted within me. My mouth is dried up like a potsherd, and my tongue sticks to the roof of my mouth; you lay me in the dust of death" (Psalm 22:14, 15).

Remember the cry of Jesus from the cross? It's recorded in John 19:28: "I thirst!" (NKJV). One thousand years earlier the psalmist had said, "My tongue sticks to the roof of my mouth."

Let's read on. "Dogs surround me; a band of villains encircles me; they pierce my hands and my feet" (Psalm 22:16). That's a prophecy about the Crucifixion. One could fasten the condemned criminal to a Roman cross in two different ways. Some were simply tied to the cross and left to die. Others were tied and nailed to the cross. How do we know that the soldiers nailed Jesus to it? that they pierced Him? Here is the testimony of Thomas, one of the disciples of Jesus: "Unless I see the nail marks in his hands and put my finger where the nails were, and put my hand into his side, I will not believe" (John 20:25). The prophecy of the psalmist, recorded 1,000 years earlier, had come to pass! "They pierce my hands and my feet."

The psalmist continued, under the inspiration of the Holy

Spirit: "All my bones are on display; people stare and gloat over me. They divide my garments among them and cast lots for my garment" (Psalm 22:17, 18).

Matthew, Mark, Luke, and John record the fulfillment of that prophecy. Here is just one testimony, that from Matthew: "When they had crucified him, they divided up his clothes by casting lots" (Matthew 27:35).

Psalm 22:19-21: "But you, Lord, do not be far from me. You are my strength; come quickly to help me. Deliver me from the sword, my precious life from the power of the dogs. Rescue me from the mouth of the lions; save me from the horns of the wild oxen."

Glorious Resurrection

At this point in the scripture song the psalmist makes an abrupt transition, beginning an entirely new theme of praise and adoration. What marks the shift from cries in the midst of suffering to words of praise and adoration? The New International Version translates verse 21 as "Rescue me from the mouth of the lions; save me from the horns of the wild oxen." But the Hebrew can also be rendered as in the New King James Version: "Save Me from the lion's mouth and from the horns of the wild oxen! You have answered Me."

"You have answered Me." The Messiah has the assurance that His cries are heard in the midst of His suffering! He catches a glimpse of what the psalmist David prophesied in

Psalm 16:9-11: "Therefore my heart is glad and my tongue rejoices; my body also will rest secure, because you will not abandon me to the realm of the dead, nor will you let your faithful one see decay. You make known to me the path of life; you will fill me with joy in your presence, with eternal pleasures at your right hand."

Here we have a clear prophesy about the Resurrection! And when the women came to the tomb early on the morning of the first day of the week, two men in clothes that gleamed like lightning said to them, "Why do you look for the living among the dead? He is not here; he has risen! Remember how he told you, while he was still with you in Galilee: 'The Son of Man must be delivered over to the hands of sinners, be crucified and on the third day be raised again.'" Then they remembered his words" (Luke 24:5-8).

My Personal Testimony

The message of one of the psalmists transformed my own life. Unlike Yasmin or Paul, I grew up in a Christian family. I often heard the name of Jesus in our home, but I lacked a personal life-changing relationship with Him. I was the captain of my own ship, master of my own destiny. Or so I thought.

Everything changed one Friday evening. My self-constructed reality came crashing down around me. Overwhelmed by external challenges and internal conflicts, I cried out to God. As I tried to pray, it seemed to me that my prayers ascended no higher than the ceiling of my bedroom. Was it too late for me? Had I damaged my soul beyond repair? In desperation I took a Bible from my bookcase and opened it. My eyes fell on an ancient psalm, and in that moment I heard the voice of God speaking directly to my heart:

> "I waited patiently for the Lord;
> And He inclined to me,
> And heard my cry.
> He also brought me up out of a horrible pit,
> Out of the miry clay,
> And set my feet upon a rock,
> And established my steps" (Psalm 40:1, 2, NKJV).

It seemed to me to be a record of my own life. Temptation. Sin. Failure. Captivity. But as I continued to read, I discovered a word of hope:

> "Let all those who seek You rejoice
> and be glad in You;
> Let such as love Your salvation say continually,
> 'The Lord be magnified!'
> But I am poor and needy;
> Yet the Lord thinks upon me.
> You are my help and my deliverer;
> Do not delay, O my God" (verses 16, 17, NKJV).

That dark night the psalmist's prayer became my own. His promise of a Deliverer became my hope. In the quiet of my room I surrendered my life fully to God and joyfully accepted the gift of His salvation. Burdens lifted. God's purpose for my life became clear.

That night I slept with peace in my heart. The following morning I received a letter in the mail. I still remember opening it. The envelope contained a small piece of blue writing paper and a stack of bank notes. The sheet of paper had a simple message: "With Christian love and God's blessings." No name. No return address. That stack of bank notes was the exact amount of money I needed to begin my studies at a Christian college in England. Four years later I graduated and entered full-time ministry as a Christian pastor. Like Yasmin, I have witnessed more miracles than I can count as I call out to God in the name of Jesus. The Lord has been faithful to His promise: "Call to Me, and I will answer you, and show you great and mighty things, which you do not know" (Jeremiah 33:3, NKJV).

Since that dark night many years ago, I have never stopped praising Jesus, my personal Savior and Friend. No wonder one of my favorite scripture songs comes from Psalm 9:

"I will praise You, O Lord, with my whole heart;
I will tell of all Your marvelous works.
I will be glad and rejoice in You;
I will sing praise to Your name, O Most High" (verses 1, 2, NKJV).

7

The Testimony of Shahbaz

A Shiite Muslim From Tehran, Iran

Shahbaz was a special child. From an early age his family called him "hajji boy" because he often spoke about God and was interested in spiritual matters. He remembers when he was 4 years old going outside his house in his hometown of Tehran, Iran, and watching the snowflakes come down. Very curious, the young Iranian boy asked himself, "Who is this God who made the snow?" He wanted to know Him better. Who is God? What does He look like?

Early Encounters With Jesus

Shahbaz had several encounters with Jesus during his childhood and young adulthood that eventually led him to accept Jesus as the true Messiah, the Son of God. The first occurred when he was 7 years old and happened by the Caspian Sea, where his father owned a summer villa. On one occasion, in the middle of the year, his family was at their villa watching an old Hollywood movie called *The Robe*. It is a 1950s film about the trial and crucifixion of Jesus. Since the movie had been dubbed into Farsi, their native tongue, they could all understand it. Toward the end of the film one of the soldiers pointed to Jesus and said, "This Man has died for the world!" Shahbaz thought to himself, *What a beautiful prophet! Why would a prophet like Jesus die for the world? How could He be such a wonderful man that He would die for the world?* He didn't know what the world had done that Jesus would come to die for it, but the boy fell in love with Jesus. Oblivious to his surroundings, Shahbaz closed his eyes and imagined meeting Jesus in a beautiful garden. Jesus appeared to him as a wonderful fatherly individual. If the movie had included an invitation for people to accept Jesus as their Savior, Shahbaz probably would have responded.

When he was 9 years old, Shahbaz felt the desire to stand up someday and preach for Allah, not in a mosque, but on the street corners. Little did he know that one day he would actually be speaking for God but in a different context.

On the Move

Shahbaz's father was a wealthy businessman in Iran, and when the boy was 11, his parents decided to buy a house in New Hampshire and move their whole family to the United States of

America. It was an exciting experience for Shahbaz and his twin brother, Shahin. They loved the yellow school buses and the Twinkie doughnuts. But at the end of one year, their mother became homesick. She didn't speak English and wanted to go back home to Iran.

Attending a Christian School

Since Shahbaz and his twin brother had learned English in the United States, their parents decided to send them to an American school north of Tehran when they returned to their homeland. It even had a yellow school bus shipped all the way from America. One beautiful August morning the family drove to the school, and Shahbaz's mother went inside to talk to the administrators. The twins waited in the car. After some time their mother returned, looking disappointed. The school was full and had no space for more students. The administrator told their mother about another English-speaking school about 15 minutes away. Shahbaz still remembers the first time he saw the school sign: Adventist School. *What is an Adventist school?* he thought to himself. He had never heard of such a thing. It was a boys' school, it did have room for more students, so their mother enrolled the twins.

They soon discovered that it was a Christian school, but 80 percent of those attending were Muslims. The Christian teachers at the school were careful not to offend any of the Muslim students. However, one person at the school was very bold—the school principal. One day, when Shahbaz's teacher was sick, the principal came to their classroom, asked the students to stand up, and then instructed them to follow him. Then he led them to the school chapel. Shahbaz had never been in a Christian chapel before. When he went inside, he was really amazed by the sight that caught his eyes: seats that could hold eight or 10 people! Having never seen a church pew before, he had always thought chairs were only for individuals.

Then the principal began to preach. It was the very first Christian sermon Shahbaz and his brother had ever heard. The principal talked about Jesus Christ. Shahbaz looked at his friends. They weren't at all interested, but he was totally captivated by everything the principal presented. The man never asked the students to accept Jesus as their Savior, but what he said about Jesus made a deep impression upon Shahbaz.

Return to the United States of America

The Iranian revolution had begun, and things had become extremely dangerous in Iran. The nation had already experienced eight months of fighting and death. Shahbaz's two older brothers and sister, who was also older, were already in America, so his parents decided that his mother would take the twin boys back to the United States. Fortunately, they still had valid U.S. visas in their passports. Two days after they left Iran the airport in Tehran closed.

Shahbaz was happy to return to the United States. He could

ride the yellow school bus again! The twins attended public school in Los Angeles, and then the family relocated to Concord in northern California. By this time Shahbaz was a little older, and even though he knew about Jesus he was more committed to Islam. He would tell his Christian classmates: first step, Judaism—failed; second step, Christianity—failed; third step, Islam—hasn't failed. That was his logic. He told his friends, "You need to become Muslims!"

First Prayer to Jesus

By the time he was 17 years old his second-oldest brother was suffering from severe schizophrenia. It was about this time Shahbaz had his next encounter with Jesus Christ. His older brother sometimes refused his medication and would become quite violent. It was one of those times. The family members tried to force him to take it, but that didn't work. Even when they begged him, he wouldn't listen. Shahbaz was desperate, because he knew if his brother went without his medication the police would take him into custody. So Shahbaz went into another room and began to pray to Allah to intervene. Although he prayed for 15 to 20 minutes, nothing happened. In his desperation he put his head on the table, and as he did a startling thought popped into his mind: *Pray to Jesus!* Pray to Jesus? Where did that idea come from? He had never prayed to Jesus. But he was so desperate that he did it. It was a simple prayer: "Jesus, make my brother take his medication." As he looked over into the other room, his brother jumped up from the couch, went into the kitchen, poured his medicine into a cup, and drank it! Shahbaz said to himself, "Wow, Jesus is powerful!" Something phenomenal happened to him that day, and he slept well with peace in his heart. While he didn't become a Christian at that time, he was learning to trust Jesus.

Jesus Draws Near

When Shahbaz was 18 years old, his mother took his older brother back to Iran. Their father had lost everything as a result of the revolution. Shahbaz remained behind in a two-bedroom apartment in Walnut Creek, California, with his remaining older brother; his twin, Shahin; and his sister. They had grown up living in an affluent home and had never needed to work before, but now the siblings had to provide for themselves. Shahbaz got a position in a fast-food restaurant, the very first job he had ever had.

One Friday night his friends invited him to go to a wild party, something he had never done before. He stayed out all night long. When he came home at 6:00 a.m. the next morning he felt terrible, having broken all the rules of his family. Guilt overwhelmed him. So he decided to pray to Allah in a Shiite Muslim custom—he bit his hand. Every time he said, "I repent," he would bite his hand again. After 10 minutes of it he could no longer feel pain in his hand, but he experienced no relief from his guilt. Then he began to bite his tongue for 10 minutes while asking Allah to forgive him, but still felt no better. Desperate and with no idea what to do, he broke down and wept for several minutes and in his native tongue asked God to forgive him. Suddenly he sensed Someone right there in his bedroom. Although he could not see this Person, Shahbaz knew He was there because the entire atmosphere of his room became thick with a holy presence. A mixture of peace, power, and love swept over him. It was so wonderful to be in that room, but he felt such a sinner that he ran out of it. He did not feel worthy to be in the midst of such holiness. Shahbaz went to his bathroom, threw some water on his face, and returned to his bedroom, but the Presence was still there. After a second trip to the bathroom, he returned to his room to find it gone. Something supernatural had occurred. Shahbaz felt free—totally relieved from his guilt for what he had done the previous night.

Searching for Help

Although he wanted to get spiritual help, Walnut Creek, California, had no mosques. He even asked a few of his Christian friends if he could speak to their pastor, but nothing ever happened. Shortly after his second encounter with Jesus, all the siblings lost their jobs in one week. Then they had to move out of their apartment as creditors repossessed all the furnishings: Persian carpets, silverware—everything. At first the family slept in the homes of their Muslim friends, and later in their cars. They were just trying to survive. Worst of all for Shahbaz, he was searching for God but didn't know where to find Him.

One day, when he was staying at a friend's house in San Mateo, he got a phone call from his twin brother, Shahin: "Shahbaz, I met a Christian man about our age out on the street, and he told me wonderful things about Jesus. I think you need to talk to him." So Shahbaz made an appointment for the next day. His plan was simple: after the man blessed him, Shahbaz would convert him to Islam!

The next afternoon he met the Christian on North Main Street in Walnut Creek. Instead of trying to tell Shahbaz what to do, the man spent about 15 minutes sharing his testimony about Jesus and what He had done for him. That morning Shahbaz had felt as if he had been locked up in a concrete box with no doors and no windows, but the testimony now touched his heart. Then the Christian spoke about the plan of salvation. As Shahbaz listened, it was as if someone were breaking up the concrete box with a hammer and allowing the light of Jesus to dispel the darkness. The man asked Shahbaz a simple question: "Will you give your heart to Jesus? Will you become a Christian today?"

"What must I do?"

"Pray with me." He asked Shahbaz to close his eyes; then he read a text from the Bible and offered a beautiful prayer.

When Shahbaz opened his eyes, the Christian reached out his hand to him and said, "Congratulations, you are a Christian now!"

"I am?" Then as he looked around, the sky seemed deeper blue than ever before. The trees appeared greener. The wind on his face felt gentler, and even the ugly people walking along the street looked beautiful! Excited, he ran back to the café where his five Muslims friends were waiting for him and said to them, "Guess what? I'm a Christian now!"

He thought they would be happy. Instead, they replied, "What? Are you crazy? Have you lost your mind? You talk to this man for 10 minutes, and you're a Christian now?" Shahbaz didn't know what to say. Although he kept silent, he knew he had experienced Christ in a living way. Jesus was alive, powerful, and able to save a sinner from any condition.

His sister found a one-bedroom apartment in Oakland, California, so they all moved in with her. They had no furniture, but they did have a TV and VCR. Shahbaz spent his time watching Christian programs on television. He also started reading a Bible someone had given him, but he had no one to teach him. One evening a Muslim friend visited their apartment. Shahbaz started telling him about his experience with Jesus. He longed for his siblings and the guest to come to know Jesus as he had. That was his greatest desire—that everyone he met would share his experience. But they all started to mock him—first their Muslim guest, and then his brothers and sister. They made fun of him and said terrible things about Jesus and about Christians. Shahbaz didn't know what to do. Instead, he just looked out the window and began to weep—both for them and for himself. He had no idea how to reach them. Going into the bedroom, he prayed, "Jesus, please help me. I'm trying to tell them about You. I want them to know You just as I have come to know You. Please take this pain from my heart, Lord. I cannot bear it."

Supernatural revelations

Shahbaz got up and went into the bathroom. As he stood there, he felt a sense of blessing flow through his body. His pain vanished, and in its place flooded a sweet love, joy, and peace. He started to weep like a little baby. Finally he came out of the bathroom speechless. When his sister saw him, she said, "What's wrong with you?" But he couldn't answer and went into the bedroom, where he had a peaceful rest.

God also gave supernatural revelations to members of Shahbaz's family. Through dreams the Lord told them, "You must do what Shahbaz has done if you are going to be in heaven." It took eight years, but eventually his twin brother Shahin became a follower of Jesus, and is serving Him as a pastor and evangelist. His sister also became a Christian and has started a radio program to tell people about Jesus. The older brother who hated Christ the most, and even cursed His name, is now also a follower of Jesus.

Compelling Testimonies

Perhaps you are wondering what happened to his parents. His mother visited him when he was living in Sweden in 1999, and he studied the Bible with her for about three months. The following year she came to visit him again after he had returned to the United States. It was not easy for her to separate from her Islamic faith. "How can I deny Islam?" she asked him. "I've been in this religion all my life." But then she said, "How can I deny Christ and all He has done for you, and all my children? He has sustained you and provided for you. He has brought you to a deeper knowledge of God and of Himself. How can I deny all these things? I want to have Jesus in my heart." She became a follower of Jesus, and even though she returned to Iran in 2001, she continues to witness openly for Christ in the marketplace. Since then she has led five other people in Iran to know Jesus as their personal Savior.

Shahbaz had very little contact with his father through the years after he became a Christian. Finally his father visited him in 2006, and Shahbaz was able to speak with him about Jesus. He showed him a series of video recordings done by Shahin and himself in the Farsi language. The father watched them intently. When he saw tears in his father's eyes, Shahbaz felt compelled to invite him to follow Jesus with all his heart. His father looked at him and said, "You know, if I accept Christ today and go back to Iran, I cannot be silent. I would probably be killed. I will come back to the United States, and then I will be baptized as a follower of Jesus." When he returned in December 2011 he was seriously ill with cancer. Shahbaz gave him three books, all in Farsi, including a book on the life of Jesus.[2]

One day, while he was reading about Jesus, he started to shake his head, closed the book, and began to sob like a baby. A flood of emotions coursed through him as he considered what Jesus had done for him. Some weeks later, while in the hospital, he asked Shahbaz's twin brother, Shahin, "Will Jesus really forgive me for everything I have done?" He listed different sins: "Will He forgive this sin? Will He forgive that sin?" Shahin assured him that "if we confess our sins, he is faithful and just and will forgive us our sins and purify us from all unrighteousness" (1 John 1:9). "Jesus, Jesus, Jesus—don't let me go." His father cried out. "Hold me, hold me, hold me!" Then he exclaimed, "He's holding me. I can feel His arms around me." His father felt himself wrapped in the arms of Jesus.

His father returned to Iran 50 days prior to his death. Although he couldn't take his Bible with him, he knew that Jesus would never leave him or forsake him. Often he would exclaim, "Sweet Jesus, sweet Jesus!" Shahbaz has no doubt in his mind that his father will see his Savior, Jesus, face to face on that glorious day when He returns in glory (see 1 Thessalonians 4:13-18).

---

[1] I have omitted Shahbaz's family name to protect his family members still living in Iran.

[2] For a free electronic copy of this remarkable book on the life and teachings of Jesus, write to dmorris@radicalevidence.com.

8

The Testimony of Cliff Goldstein

A Secular Jew From Miami Beach, Florida

How could a self-proclaimed "hard-core philosophical materialist" who hated Christians ever come to believe in Jesus as the way, the truth, and the life?[1] Such a radical life transformation would require a miraculous intervention by God.

Cliff was raised in a secular Jewish home and educated in a postmodern secular environment. "I grew up on Miami Beach and went to a high school where everyone was either Jewish or stoned, or both, and where I learned nothing about religion, either my own or anyone else's. The only time I ever spoke the name of Jesus was as a curse." He was taught that everything is relative. Only a person's culture, education, and individual choices determine right and wrong and morality.

There is no God's-eye view of things to stand above and judge what is truly right and truly wrong. Each person has to decide for himself or herself.

Cliff's Search for Truth

One day, when Cliff was 21, he was sitting in a pizza parlor in Gainesville, Florida, reading a book by Benedict de Spinoza. The author challenged his readers to discover the answer to the question "Why am I here?" and to live life accordingly. That thought penetrated Cliff's mind and began to shape his life. "Why am I here?" There must be some reason. Truth has to exist.

As he looked at the pizza in front of him, Cliff realized that a thousand people could give a thousand different explanations as to how it got there. Someone might believe the Babylonian god Marduk made the pizza. Another might announce that aliens from Venus traveled through space in a flying saucer and put the pizza there. Some might have believed it just evolved. Others, that it even created itself. There could be a thousand views out there on the origin and meaning of the pizza, views that people would be willing to die for or even to kill for. But Cliff realized that not all of those explanations could be right. In fact, all of them might be wrong. But the fact remained that somewhere out there the explanation for the pizza did exist (even if no one knew what it was), and that that explanation was the truth about the pizza.

Suddenly Cliff realized that, in the same way as there existed a truth to account for the pizza, there had to be one that explained the cosmos and human existence—and that whatever it was, it would be *The Truth*. He then decided, right there in the pizza parlor, that he wanted to know that Truth if it was humanly possible. Cliff didn't care where it took him, what it cost, or what he had to suffer.

As he left the pizza parlor that night, a thought burned inside him: *If it is possible to know this truth about my origins, about my existence, then I want to know it wherever it leads me, whatever it costs me, or what I have to suffer or give up because of it. If I could ever know it, I want to know it—no matter what.*

During the next few years he searched for that Truth in many places: philosophy, Eastern religions, Marxism. "Show Your face if You have one, if You dare," he once challenged God.

Animosity Toward Christians

There was one group Cliff hated—Christians. Even though he wasn't a religious Jew, he was bitter about all the persecution that Jews had suffered at the hands of professed Christians. He had read about the Crusaders who entered Jerusalem, rounded up all the Jewish men, women, and children, herded them into a synagogue, and burned them alive. That persecution of Jews by "Christians" had continued down through the ages: the Inquisition, pogroms in Russia, anti-Semitism in its many ugly forms. Cliff used to vent his anger on a Christian preacher named Jed Smock, who came to the University of

Florida campus in Gainesville, Florida. His university friends gave Cliff the nickname "Heckle," because he would harass that Christian preacher when the man tried to share his convictions about God. More than one preacher told Cliff there was no hope for his soul, that he was damned and going to hell.

A Passion for Writing

Cliff graduated from college in 1978 with a single goal: he wanted to be a novelist. Writing was in his genes: "If you shook my family tree, pens, pencils, typewriters, and books would clatter to the ground, followed by reams of fluttering manuscripts, magazines, and newspapers. I have generations of writers in my blood, and whatever inspired them pulses through me, too." While still a senior in college he started working on his first novel. All that mattered to him was writing that book. It was his obsession. "I kept writing, furiously writing, pouring all my soul into every sentence, paragraph, and page. The novel was the center of my life. Everything else was peripheral."

Searching for Inspiration

He decided to use some of his limited savings to travel to England so that he could work on his novel. There he spent a few days in a Cistercian monastery on Caldey Island off the Welsh coast until the monks evicted him from the island for getting drunk. Then he hitchhiked through Wales and England, caught a boat across the English Channel, and made his way to

Greece in the hope of meeting a friend there. When he finally arrived in Athens, he discovered his friend was thousands of miles away, visiting Cliff's hometown of Miami, Florida!

Discouraged, with nowhere to stay and not much money left, he rolled out his sleeping bag under some bushes and settled down for the night. While he was sleeping, this hard-core philosophical materialist had a dream: in it he booked a ticket to Israel so that he could live on a Jewish collective community (kibbutz) and work on his novel.[2] When he awoke the next morning, he decided to follow his dream. He went across the street to a travel agent, bought a ticket to Israel, and before long he was living on a kibbutz in Galilee. Although expected to work 30 hours a week, he had the rest of the time available for writing. Nothing else mattered. His novel was his life. "At least here there will be no Christians to harass me," he reasoned.

But Cliff had been working at the kibbutz for only one week when a group of Christians arrived from America. Furious at their presence, he began harassing them: "I started in on them immediately, and yet no matter what abuse and blasphemy came out of my loud, dirty mouth, these people showed me continual kindness and love." It got so bad that the people on the kibbutz threatened to throw him out. Then another Christian arrived, but he was different from the rest. He was a Jew who believed in Jesus. Now Cliff was really angry, so he started haranguing him, but the man was deep and highly intelligent. Having grown up believing the Bible was a collection of Late

Bronze Age camel herder myths, Cliff couldn't understand how anyone who was intelligent and educated could believe in the Bible as an inspired revelation from God, but his deep discussions with the Jewish Christian really made him think.

After about a year, Cliff left the kibbutz and traveled to Denmark. He spent a few days at a large commune called Christiania, but after a fight with someone who threatened him with a knife, Cliff connected with an old friend deeply involved with the occult. It was obvious the man was extremely troubled. One day, when his friend was having a particularly bad day, Cliff said something to him about Jesus. "I don't know why Jesus came to my mind, because I surely didn't believe in Him," he remembers.

Crying Out for Help

Eventually Cliff left Copenhagen and headed south to Paris. His life heading downhill, he even considered jumping off the Eiffel Tower. As soon as he had that suicidal thought, another one passed through his mind: "Hang on, because maybe this Jesus stuff is true." Cliff felt angry with himself at that moment for even considering the idea. After all, religion was for weak people who couldn't handle life. But in desperation Cliff looked up in the sky and said, "OK, God, if You're there, if You exist, You have to reveal Yourself to me. Otherwise, I'm never going to believe." He needed a miraculous intervention by God.

From Paris, Cliff returned to Israel, but they wouldn't let him back into the kibbutz. He told some of the Christians there, "I'm open, but God has to reveal Himself to me."

"'You ask, He'll respond," one of them told him. Someone gave him a Bible, and the Christians even baptized him in the Jordan River, but he still didn't know Jesus or have any relationship with Him. "I was no more born again than a corpse," he recalls.

Dangerous Deceptions

Before he left Israel, Cliff experienced some unusual sensations—tingling in his toes and the strange feeling of moving through a wind tunnel. He remembers sitting up and thinking, *What was that?* It happened again after he returned to the United States. One afternoon when he had lain down to take a nap he felt the same tingling in his toes and pounding in his head. This time he decided not to resist. Suddenly he felt himself going right out of his body and through the roof. He didn't know what was happening, but it felt real. After that experience he decided to start studying the occult. Perhaps his spiritualist friend in Copenhagen was on to something.

The next day Cliff went to the library to find a book on spiritualism. On his way there he stopped at a health food store. When Cliff mentioned his interest in the occult, an employee at the store tried to warn him about the dangers of spiritualism. He even gave Cliff a book to read: *The Great Controversy.* That book would answer many of his questions about Truth and reality.[3]

Encounter With Jesus

Several days later Cliff was sitting in his room with his fingers on the typewriter. As he mused about his precious novel, the presence of Jesus entered his room. In that instant Cliff knew exactly who He was and what He wanted. "For months the Holy Spirit had been quietly convicting me that my commitment to Christ must be total, absolute, and that my fervent, unwavering devotion toward the book needed to be directed toward God alone."

That night, in his ramshackle room in Gainesville, Florida, Jesus said to him, "Cliff, you have been playing with Me long enough. If you want Me tonight, burn the novel." He revealed to Cliff that his novel was his god.

"Please, God," Cliff pleaded, "let me finish the book, and then I'll give my life to You. I'll rewrite it all to Your glory, but let me keep it." Finally he said, "Let me just put it away for a while." He had poured his entire life into that book—in fact, it was his life. Jumping up, he burst into tears and hurried out of the room. After running through the streets of Gainesville, he finally stopped under a streetlamp. "OK, God, I want You and I want Truth more than I want this book. But I just don't have it in me to burn it. If You want it burned, You'll have to do it Yourself."

The moment Cliff made that choice, the burden lifted. Returning to his room, he destroyed his precious novel. "In an hour all that remained of two years' work lay scattered on my front porch, smoldering like war ruins. The battle was over. I had surrendered unconditionally." And that night all Cliff's occult experiences ceased. The words of the apostle John were fulfilled in Cliff's life: "You, dear children, are from God and have overcome them, because the one who is in you is greater than the one who is in the world" (1 John 4:4).

Writing With a Mission

When Cliff burned his novel that night, he thought he might never write again—and he was fine with that. He had died completely not only to the book but to writing itself. If that is what it took, the price was cheap enough.

For about two years he didn't do any writing. Then one day the door opened for him to prepare an article, which he did. Now more than 22 books later, Cliff is still writing. But he does so with passion about a new message—the good news about Jesus. He is a transformed witness with a compelling testimony. He doesn't live for his books anymore. Cliff lives for Jesus, who rescued him from a meaningless life and delivered him from certain death.

---

[1] This radical claim of Jesus is recorded in John 14:6.

[2] A kibbutz is a collective community in Israel. Kibbutzim began as utopian communities based on a mixture of socialism and Zionism. Currently Israel has more than 200 of them.

[3] For a free electronic copy of this remarkable account of the cosmic struggle between good and evil, write to dmorris@radicalevidence.com.

Epilogue

The two disciples on the Emmaus road could not keep the good news about Jesus to themselves: "They got up and returned at once to Jerusalem. There they found the Eleven and those with them, assembled together and saying, 'It is true! The Lord has risen and has appeared to Simon.' Then the two told what had happened on the way, and how Jesus was recognized by them when he broke the bread" (Luke 24:33-35). Yasmin, Paul, Shahbaz, and Cliff have done the same—they have become passionate witnesses for Jesus.

I challenge you to follow their example: share with others the Truth you have embraced. Send a copy of this book to someone who is searching for meaning and purpose in life. Invite some friends to start a study group.* Give your own compelling testimony. You have light to share.

I close with the words of Jesus to each one who has come to know Him as "the radiance of God's glory and the exact representation of his being" (Hebrews 1:3): "You are the light of the world. A town built on a hill cannot be hidden. Neither do people light a lamp and put it under a bowl. Instead they put it on its stand, and it gives light to everyone in the house" (Matthew 5:14).

May the Light of the world shine through you as you declare "the praises of Him who called you out of darkness into His marvelous light" (1 Peter 2:9).

---

* A companion DVD and small group study guides are available at www.radicalevidence.com.

Discussion Questions for Small-Group Study

Chapter 1: The Testimony of Yasmin Sultana

1. Where do you see the first evidence of God's leading in Yasmin's life?

2. What does it mean to pray "in the name of Jesus" (see John 14:13)?

3. What experiences with prayer have convinced you that Jesus is a prayer-answering Savior?

Chapter 2: The Testimony of Paul Ratsara

1. What experiences in your life has God used to show you your great need of Him?

2. Some people read the Gospels and get nothing out of them. In contrast, Matthew's inspired testimony about Jesus transformed Paul's heart. What makes the difference?

3. How can you experience freedom from fear and holy
    boldness as a follower of Jesus?

Chapter 3: The Testimony of Cleopas

1. What disappointments in your life have caused you to
    question your faith in Jesus as Messiah?
2. What part of the Emmaus road story affects you most
    profoundly?
3. How have you handled the truth that has been revealed
    to you about Jesus?

Chapter 4: The Testimony of Moses

1. Why do you think Jesus began His Bible study with the
    inspired testimony of Moses?
2. What important lesson do you glean from the story of
    the fiery serpents in the wilderness (Numbers 21:4-9)?
3. When did you decide to look to Jesus and live? If you have
    not yet made that decision, what's holding you back?

Chapter 5: The Testimony of the Prophets

1. Many liberal scholars deny that any of the prophecies
    of the Old Testament point directly to Jesus as the
    Messiah. What evidence in the teachings of Jesus
    and the apostles confirms that the prophets do indeed
    provide compelling testimonies regarding Jesus as
    Messiah?

2. Which prophecy concerning Jesus as Messiah impresses you the most?

3. Who has encouraged or helped you to believe the testimony of Scripture regarding Jesus as the true Messiah?

Chapter 6: The Testimony of the Psalmists

1. Which of the psalms is your favorite? Why?

2. What portion of Psalm 22 affected you the most in reference to Jesus as the Messiah?

3. What are some ways you can share the truth about Jesus with others?

Chapter 7: The Testimony of Shahbaz

1. Why did God reveal Himself to Shahbaz through dreams and supernatural manifestations?

2. Why was it such a struggle for some of Shahbaz's family members to accept Jesus as the true Messiah?

3. How does confidence in Jesus as your Messiah enable you to face death unafraid?

Chapter 8: The Testimony of Cliff Goldstein

1. What god has tried to take first place in your life?

2. What prejudices hindered you, or still hold you back, from fully embracing Jesus as your personal Savior?

3. What is the most important lesson you learn from Cliff's testimony for your life today?